I0765955

Get A Free Book At: xspurts.com/posts/free-book-offer

Table of Contents

Integral Theory also introduces the concept of levels of development, which describe the stages of growth and evolution that individuals, cultures, and societies pass through. These levels range from archaic to integral and describe increasingly complex ways of organizing and understanding the world. By acknowledging the existence of multiple levels of development, Integral Theory provides a nuanced understanding of human behavior and societal dynamics.

Another key component of Integral Theory is the concept of lines of development. These lines represent different aspects of human potential that can be cultivated and developed over time, including cognitive intelligence, emotional intelligence, moral development, and aesthetic sensitivity. Integral Theory emphasizes the importance of addressing all lines of development for holistic personal growth and development.

Integral Theory also emphasizes the significance of states of consciousness, which are different ways of experiencing reality. These states can vary from waking consciousness to deep meditative states and altered states induced by psychedelics. Integral Theory recognizes the value of diverse spiritual experiences and practices, advocating for spiritual practices such as meditation and contemplation as essential for personal growth and development.

Integral Theory has applications in various fields, including psychology, education, business, and spirituality. In psychology, Integral Theory provides a comprehensive framework for understanding human behavior and mental health, integrating insights from psychoanalysis, behaviorism, and transpersonal psychology. In education, Integral Theory advocates for a holistic approach to learning that addresses the cognitive, emotional, and spiritual dimensions of education. In business, Integral Theory emphasizes the importance of considering multiple stakeholders and balancing competing interests to achieve sustainable and ethical outcomes. In spirituality, Integral Theory offers a framework for integrating different religious and mystical traditions, recognizing the validity of diverse spiritual experiences and practices.

In conclusion, Integral Theory offers a holistic perspective on reality that integrates insights from various disciplines and perspectives. By recognizing the interconnectedness of all phenomena and the importance of addressing multiple dimensions simultaneously, Integral Theory provides a powerful tool for personal and social transformation. Whether applied to individual development, organizational change, or global challenges, Integral Theory offers a roadmap for navigating the complexities of the modern world.

Origins and contributors of Integral Theory

Origins and Contributors of Integral Theory

Integral Theory, a comprehensive framework for understanding reality, emerged from the works of various thinkers and scholars, with philosopher Ken Wilber being the most prominent figure associated with its development. However, Integral Theory's roots can be traced back to several key influences and contributors, each adding their unique insights to the evolution of this interdisciplinary approach.

One of the foundational influences on Integral Theory is the work of the American philosopher and psychologist William James. James explored the nature of consciousness, religious experience, and the relationship between the individual and the universe. His ideas laid the groundwork for understanding the importance of subjective experience and the diverse ways in which individuals perceive reality.

Another significant influence on Integral Theory is the Swiss psychiatrist Carl Jung. Jung's concepts of archetypes, the collective unconscious, and the process of individuation provided valuable insights into the psychological dimensions of human existence. Jung's work emphasized the importance of integrating the various aspects of the psyche to achieve wholeness and self-realization, a theme that resonates deeply within Integral Theory.

The American psychologist Abraham Maslow also made significant contributions to Integral Theory through his research on human motivation and self-actualization. Maslow's hierarchy of needs and his concept of peak experiences highlighted the importance of personal growth and self-transcendence in the quest for fulfillment. Maslow's ideas influenced Integral Theory's emphasis on human development and the exploration of higher states of consciousness.

Integral Theory also draws inspiration from the field of systems theory, particularly the work of biologist Ludwig von Bertalanffy. Bertalanffy's ideas about the interconnectedness of systems and the principles of hierarchy and holism provided a framework for understanding the complex interactions between different levels of reality. Integral Theory incorporates systems thinking into its approach, recognizing the interdependence of individual, social, and ecological systems.

The contributions of Eastern philosophy and spirituality have also played a significant role in shaping Integral Theory. Eastern traditions such as Hinduism, Buddhism, and Taoism offer insights into the nature of consciousness, the interconnectedness of all things, and the quest for enlightenment. Integral Theory integrates these perspectives into its framework, acknowledging the value of contemplative practices and mystical experiences in the pursuit of wholeness and integration.

However, it is Ken Wilber who is most closely associated with the development and popularization of Integral Theory. Wilber's seminal work, "A Theory of Everything," and subsequent writings have synthesized the insights of various disciplines into a coherent framework for understanding reality. Wilber's Integral Model incorporates elements from psychology, philosophy, science, spirituality, and sociology, offering a comprehensive perspective that transcends disciplinary boundaries.

In conclusion, Integral Theory has its origins in the works of diverse thinkers and scholars who explored the nature of consciousness, human development, systems theory, and spirituality. Through the contributions of figures such as William James, Carl Jung, Abraham Maslow, Ludwig von Bertalanffy, and Ken Wilber, Integral Theory has evolved into a comprehensive framework for understanding the complexities of existence. By integrating insights from multiple disciplines and perspectives, Integral Theory offers a holistic approach to personal and social transformation, providing a roadmap for navigating the complexities of the modern world.

Core Concepts in Integral Theory

Core Concepts in Integral Theory

Integral Theory, a comprehensive framework for understanding reality developed by philosopher Ken Wilber, is built upon several core concepts that provide the foundation for its holistic approach. These concepts, ranging from quadrants and levels to lines of development and states of consciousness, offer insights into the interconnected nature of existence and the complexity of human experience.

One of the fundamental concepts in Integral Theory is the notion of quadrants. These quadrants represent four distinct perspectives through which reality can be understood: the individual interior (I), the individual exterior (IT), the collective interior (WE), and the collective exterior (ITS). By acknowledging the importance of subjective experience, behavior, culture, and social systems, Integral Theory emphasizes the need to consider multiple dimensions simultaneously.

Integral Theory also introduces the concept of levels of development, which describe the stages of growth and evolution that individuals, cultures, and societies pass through. These levels, which range from archaic to integral, represent increasingly complex ways of organizing and understanding the world. By recognizing the existence of multiple levels of development, Integral Theory provides a nuanced understanding of human behavior and societal dynamics.

Another key component of Integral Theory is the concept of lines of development. These lines represent different aspects of human potential that can be cultivated and developed over time, including cognitive intelligence, emotional intelligence, moral development, and aesthetic sensitivity. Integral Theory emphasizes the importance of addressing all lines of development for holistic personal growth and development.

Integral Theory also emphasizes the significance of states of consciousness, which are different ways of experiencing reality. These states can vary from waking consciousness to deep meditative states and altered states induced by psychedelics. Integral Theory recognizes the value of diverse spiritual experiences and practices, advocating for spiritual practices such as meditation and contemplation as essential for personal growth and development.

Integral Theory's integral model incorporates all of these core concepts into a coherent framework for understanding reality. By integrating insights from various disciplines and perspectives, Integral Theory offers a comprehensive approach to personal and social transformation. Whether applied to individual development, organizational change, or global challenges, Integral Theory provides a roadmap for navigating the complexities of the modern world.

In conclusion, Integral Theory is built upon several core concepts that provide a foundation for its holistic approach to understanding reality. From quadrants and levels to lines of development and states of consciousness, these concepts offer insights into the interconnected nature of existence and the complexity of human experience. By integrating insights from various disciplines and perspectives, Integral Theory offers a comprehensive framework for personal and social transformation, providing a roadmap for navigating the complexities of the modern world.

Integral Methodological Pluralism

Integral Methodological Pluralism: Embracing Diversity in Inquiry

Integral Theory, spearheaded by philosopher Ken Wilber, encompasses a broad range of perspectives and approaches to understanding reality. One of its core principles, Integral Methodological Pluralism (IMP), emphasizes the importance of employing multiple methods and approaches in inquiry. This approach acknowledges the diverse nature of phenomena and the limitations of any single method in capturing the complexity of reality.

Integral Methodological Pluralism recognizes that different phenomena may require different methods of investigation. For example, subjective experiences may be best explored through introspection and qualitative research methods, while objective phenomena may be more effectively studied using quantitative measures and empirical observation. By embracing a variety of methods, researchers can gain a more comprehensive understanding of the phenomena under investigation.

Integral Methodological Pluralism also emphasizes the importance of integrating insights from multiple disciplines and perspectives. Rather than privileging one approach over others, IMP encourages researchers to draw from a wide range of disciplines, including psychology, sociology, anthropology, biology, and spirituality. By integrating diverse perspectives, researchers can develop a more nuanced understanding of complex phenomena and avoid the limitations of disciplinary silos.

Integral Methodological Pluralism is closely related to Integral Theory's emphasis on quadrants, levels, lines, and states. Each of these dimensions of reality may require different methods of investigation, and Integral Methodological Pluralism provides a framework for selecting and integrating appropriate methods. For example, the interior dimensions of consciousness and subjective experience may be best explored using methods such as meditation, psychotherapy, or phenomenological inquiry, while the exterior dimensions of behavior and social systems may be more effectively studied using methods such as empirical observation, statistical analysis, or systems theory.

Integral Methodological Pluralism has implications for both research and practice in various fields. In psychology, for example, researchers may employ a combination of qualitative and quantitative methods to explore the complexities of human behavior and mental health. In education, teachers may draw from multiple pedagogical approaches to address the diverse needs of students. In business, managers may integrate insights from psychology, economics, and organizational theory to develop effective strategies for leadership and decision-making.

Integral Methodological Pluralism also has implications for personal and social transformation. By embracing diverse perspectives and methods, individuals can develop a more comprehensive understanding of themselves and the world around them. This can lead to greater empathy, compassion, and collaboration, fostering positive change at both the individual and collective levels.

However, Integral Methodological Pluralism is not without its challenges. Integrating diverse perspectives and methods requires openness, flexibility, and a willingness to engage in interdisciplinary dialogue. It also requires careful consideration of the strengths and limitations of different methods and the potential biases that may arise from their use.

In conclusion, Integral Methodological Pluralism offers a framework for embracing diversity in inquiry. By employing multiple methods and integrating insights from various disciplines and perspectives, researchers can develop a more comprehensive understanding of complex phenomena. This approach has implications for research, practice, and personal transformation, offering a pathway to greater insight, empathy, and collaboration in the quest for knowledge and understanding.

Understanding Methodological Pluralism

Understanding Methodological Pluralism: Embracing Diversity in Inquiry

Methodological pluralism is a concept that underscores the importance of employing a variety of research methods and approaches in the pursuit of knowledge and understanding. It acknowledges that no single method is capable of fully capturing the complexities of reality and that different methods may be better suited to exploring different aspects of a phenomenon. Methodological pluralism is particularly emphasized in Integral Theory, a comprehensive framework developed by philosopher Ken Wilber, which encourages researchers to draw from a diverse range of disciplines and perspectives in their inquiry.

At its core, methodological pluralism recognizes that reality is multifaceted and cannot be fully understood through any single lens. Instead, it advocates for the integration of multiple perspectives and approaches to gain a more comprehensive understanding of complex phenomena. This approach is especially relevant in fields such as psychology, sociology, and anthropology, where human behavior and social dynamics are influenced by a wide range of factors.

One of the key benefits of methodological pluralism is its ability to uncover deeper insights and perspectives that may be overlooked by a single method. For example, while quantitative methods such as surveys and experiments can provide valuable statistical data, they may fail to capture the subjective experiences and cultural nuances that qualitative methods such as interviews and ethnography can uncover. By combining quantitative and qualitative approaches, researchers can gain a more holistic understanding of the phenomenon under investigation.

Methodological pluralism also encourages interdisciplinary collaboration, recognizing that different disciplines may offer unique insights into a particular phenomenon. By drawing from fields such as psychology, sociology, biology, and philosophy, researchers can enrich their understanding and develop more nuanced theories and explanations. This interdisciplinary approach is central to Integral Theory, which seeks to integrate insights from various disciplines to create a more comprehensive framework for understanding reality.

However, methodological pluralism is not without its challenges. Integrating multiple methods and perspectives requires careful consideration of their strengths and limitations, as well as the potential biases that may arise from their use. Researchers must also navigate the complexities of interdisciplinary collaboration, including differences in terminology, methodology, and theoretical frameworks.

Despite these challenges, methodological pluralism offers a pathway to greater depth and richness in inquiry. By embracing diversity in methods and perspectives, researchers can develop more nuanced theories and explanations that better reflect the complexity of reality. This approach is essential for addressing the complex challenges facing society today, from climate change and social inequality to mental health and well-being.

In conclusion, methodological pluralism is a foundational principle in the pursuit of knowledge and understanding. By embracing diversity in methods and perspectives, researchers can uncover deeper insights and develop more comprehensive theories and explanations. This approach is particularly emphasized in Integral Theory, which encourages researchers to draw from a wide range of disciplines and perspectives in their inquiry. By integrating multiple methods and perspectives, researchers can gain a more holistic understanding of complex phenomena and contribute to positive change in the world.

Importance in Integral Theory

Importance in Integral Theory

Integral Theory, a comprehensive framework developed by philosopher Ken Wilber, holds significant importance in the realms of philosophy, psychology, sociology, spirituality, and beyond. This approach to understanding reality emphasizes the interconnectedness of all phenomena and encourages the integration of diverse perspectives and methodologies. Integral Theory's importance lies in its ability to provide a holistic framework for addressing complex challenges and fostering personal and societal transformation.

One of the key aspects of Integral Theory is its emphasis on inclusivity and integration. By recognizing the validity of multiple perspectives and approaches, Integral Theory seeks to transcend the limitations of narrow disciplinary boundaries. This integrative approach allows researchers and practitioners to draw from a wide range of disciplines and methodologies, enriching their understanding and enhancing the effectiveness of their work.

Integral Theory also provides a comprehensive framework for understanding human development and consciousness. By incorporating insights from psychology, sociology, and spirituality, Integral Theory offers a nuanced understanding of the stages of growth and evolution that individuals, cultures, and societies pass through. This understanding is essential for fostering personal growth and well-being and addressing the complex challenges facing humanity.

Integral Theory's emphasis on interconnectedness and integration is particularly relevant in today's increasingly interconnected world. By recognizing the interdependence of all phenomena, Integral Theory offers insights into the dynamics of global systems and the interconnected nature of environmental, social, and economic issues. This holistic perspective is essential for addressing complex challenges such as climate change, poverty, and social inequality.

Furthermore, Integral Theory provides a framework for personal and societal transformation. By integrating insights from psychology, spirituality, and philosophy, Integral Theory offers guidance for individuals seeking to cultivate greater self-awareness, compassion, and wisdom. At the societal level, Integral Theory offers insights into the dynamics of cultural evolution and the potential for collective growth and development.

Integral Theory's emphasis on inclusivity and integration is also reflected in its approach to spirituality. By recognizing the validity of diverse spiritual traditions and practices, Integral Theory offers a framework for integrating spiritual insights into daily life. This integrative approach to spirituality is essential for fostering a sense of connection, meaning, and purpose in an increasingly secular world.

In conclusion, Integral Theory holds significant importance in the realms of philosophy, psychology, sociology, spirituality, and beyond. By emphasizing inclusivity, integration, and interconnectedness, Integral Theory offers a holistic framework for understanding reality and addressing complex challenges. This integrative approach is essential for fostering personal and societal transformation and navigating the complexities of the modern world. Integral Theory's emphasis on inclusivity, integration, and interconnectedness makes it a valuable tool for individuals and societies seeking to cultivate greater self-awareness, compassion, and wisdom in an increasingly interconnected world.

Applications of Methodological Pluralism

Applications of Methodological Pluralism

Methodological pluralism, the practice of employing a diverse range of research methods and approaches, finds extensive applications across various disciplines and fields, including but not limited to psychology, sociology, anthropology, and ecology. Rooted in the philosophy of Integral Theory, which emphasizes the integration of diverse perspectives, methodological pluralism allows researchers to gain a more comprehensive understanding of complex phenomena and address multifaceted challenges. Here, we explore some key applications of methodological pluralism and its significance in advancing knowledge and fostering innovation.

In psychology, methodological pluralism is essential for exploring the complexities of human behavior and mental processes. Researchers employ a variety of methods, including experiments, surveys, interviews, and observational studies, to investigate different aspects of cognition, emotion, and social interaction. By integrating quantitative and qualitative approaches, psychologists can gain deeper insights into phenomena such as personality, motivation, and mental health, leading to more effective interventions and treatments.

Similarly, in sociology, methodological pluralism allows researchers to study the complexities of social structures, processes, and dynamics. Sociologists may use methods such as ethnography, surveys, and archival research to explore topics ranging from social inequality and deviance to culture and globalization. By employing a variety of methods, sociologists can uncover hidden patterns, understand diverse perspectives, and contribute to social change and justice.

Methodological pluralism also finds applications in anthropology, where researchers study human societies and cultures from a holistic perspective. Anthropologists may use methods such as participant observation, interviews, and archival research to explore cultural beliefs, practices, and customs. By combining qualitative and quantitative approaches, anthropologists can gain a deeper understanding of cultural diversity and human adaptation, contributing to cross-cultural understanding and collaboration.

In ecology, methodological pluralism allows researchers to study the complexities of ecosystems and environmental processes. Ecologists may use methods such as field experiments, remote sensing, and mathematical modeling to investigate ecological patterns and processes. By integrating data from different sources and scales, ecologists can assess the impacts of human activities, inform conservation efforts, and promote sustainability.

Moreover, methodological pluralism has applications in interdisciplinary research, where researchers draw from multiple disciplines and perspectives to address complex challenges. For example, in public health, researchers may combine insights from epidemiology, sociology, and psychology to study the determinants of health and develop interventions to improve population health. By integrating diverse perspectives and methods, interdisciplinary research can generate innovative solutions to pressing societal issues.

In conclusion, methodological pluralism plays a vital role in advancing knowledge and fostering innovation across various disciplines and fields. By embracing diversity in methods and perspectives, researchers can gain a more comprehensive understanding of complex phenomena and address multifaceted challenges. Rooted in the philosophy of Integral Theory, methodological pluralism underscores the importance of integration, inclusivity, and interdisciplinary collaboration in the pursuit of knowledge and understanding. As researchers continue to navigate the complexities of the modern world, methodological pluralism remains a valuable tool for promoting discovery, creativity, and positive change.

Quadrants in Integral Theory

Quadrants in Integral Theory

Integral Theory, a comprehensive framework developed by philosopher Ken Wilber, offers a unique perspective on understanding reality by incorporating multiple dimensions and perspectives. One of the key concepts within Integral Theory is that of quadrants. These quadrants represent four fundamental perspectives through which reality can be viewed, providing a lens to analyze complex phenomena in a holistic manner.

The first quadrant, referred to as the individual interior (I), focuses on the subjective experiences and consciousness of individuals. This quadrant encompasses the inner world of thoughts, emotions, beliefs, and intentions. It explores the psychological dimensions of human existence, including personal values, worldviews, and spiritual experiences. Through methods such as introspection, meditation, and psychotherapy, researchers gain insight into the inner workings of the mind and the subjective experiences that shape human behavior.

The second quadrant, the individual exterior (IT), examines the observable behaviors and physiological processes of individuals. This quadrant encompasses the outer world of actions, behaviors, and biological functions. It explores the physical dimensions of human existence, including bodily movements, brain activity, and genetic predispositions. Through methods such as observation, experimentation, and neuroimaging, researchers gain insight into the external manifestations of behavior and the underlying physiological mechanisms.

The third quadrant, the collective interior (WE), focuses on the shared values, norms, and cultural practices of groups and communities. This quadrant encompasses the inner world of collective beliefs, identities, and social norms. It explores the cultural dimensions of human existence, including shared meanings, rituals, and traditions. Through methods such as ethnography, cultural studies, and discourse analysis, researchers gain insight into the cultural dynamics that shape collective identity and behavior.

The fourth quadrant, the collective exterior (ITS), examines the observable structures and systems of groups and societies. This quadrant encompasses the outer world of social institutions, organizations, and material environments. It explores the social dimensions of human existence, including economic systems, political institutions, and built environments. Through methods such as social network analysis, institutional analysis, and urban planning, researchers gain insight into the external structures that shape collective behavior and social organization.

Integral Theory emphasizes the interconnectedness of these four quadrants and the importance of considering all perspectives simultaneously. By integrating insights from the individual and collective, interior and exterior dimensions, Integral Theory provides a comprehensive framework for understanding the complexities of reality. This holistic approach allows researchers to analyze complex phenomena from multiple angles, leading to a deeper understanding of the underlying dynamics and interrelations.

Furthermore, Integral Theory suggests that each quadrant can influence and interact with the others, leading to emergent properties and dynamics. For example, changes in individual consciousness (quadrant I) may lead to shifts in social norms and cultural practices (quadrant III), which in turn may influence the structures and institutions of society (quadrant IV). By considering these interrelations, Integral Theory offers insights into the dynamics of change and transformation at both the individual and collective levels.

In conclusion, quadrants play a crucial role in Integral Theory, providing a framework for analyzing the complexities of reality from multiple perspectives. By considering the individual and collective, interior and exterior dimensions, researchers gain a more comprehensive understanding of the interconnectedness of all phenomena. This holistic approach allows for a deeper analysis of complex phenomena and provides insights into the dynamics of change and transformation in individuals, communities, and societies.

Defining the Quadrants

Defining the Quadrants in Integral Theory

Integral Theory, a comprehensive framework developed by philosopher Ken Wilber, introduces the concept of quadrants as a fundamental aspect of understanding reality. These quadrants provide a multidimensional lens through which complex phenomena can be analyzed, offering insights into the interconnected nature of individual and collective existence. Let's delve into the four quadrants and explore their unique characteristics and contributions to Integral Theory.

The first quadrant, known as the individual interior (I), focuses on the subjective experiences and consciousness of individuals. This quadrant delves into the inner world of thoughts, emotions, beliefs, and intentions. It encompasses the psychological dimensions of human existence, including personal values, worldviews, and spiritual experiences. Through introspection, meditation, and psychotherapy, researchers gain insight into the inner workings of the mind and the subjective experiences that shape human behavior.

Moving to the second quadrant, the individual exterior (IT) examines the observable behaviors and physiological processes of individuals. This quadrant explores the outer world of actions, behaviors, and biological functions. It encompasses the physical dimensions of human existence, including bodily movements, brain activity, and genetic predispositions. Through observation, experimentation, and neuroimaging, researchers gain insight into the external manifestations of behavior and the underlying physiological mechanisms.

Transitioning to the third quadrant, the collective interior (WE) zooms in on the shared values, norms, and cultural practices of groups and communities. This quadrant explores the inner world of collective beliefs, identities, and social norms. It delves into the cultural dimensions of human existence, including shared meanings, rituals, and traditions. Through ethnography, cultural studies, and discourse analysis, researchers gain insight into the cultural dynamics that shape collective identity and behavior.

Finally, the fourth quadrant, the collective exterior (ITS), examines the observable structures and systems of groups and societies. This quadrant encompasses the outer world of social institutions, organizations, and material environments. It explores the social dimensions of human existence, including economic systems, political institutions, and built environments. Through social network analysis, institutional analysis, and urban planning, researchers gain insight into the external structures that shape collective behavior and social organization.

Integral Theory emphasizes the interconnectedness of these four quadrants and the importance of considering all perspectives simultaneously. By integrating insights from the individual and collective, interior and exterior dimensions, Integral Theory provides a comprehensive framework for understanding the complexities of reality. This holistic approach allows researchers to analyze complex phenomena from multiple angles, leading to a deeper understanding of the underlying dynamics and interrelations.

Furthermore, Integral Theory suggests that each quadrant interacts with and influences the others, leading to emergent properties and dynamics. For example, changes in individual consciousness (quadrant I) may impact social norms and cultural practices (quadrant III), which in turn may influence the structures and institutions of society (quadrant IV). By considering these interrelations, Integral Theory offers insights into the dynamics of change and transformation at both the individual and collective levels.

In conclusion, the quadrants in Integral Theory provide a multidimensional framework for understanding reality. By considering the individual and collective, interior and exterior dimensions, researchers gain a more comprehensive understanding of the interconnectedness of all phenomena. This holistic approach allows for a deeper analysis of complex phenomena and provides insights into the dynamics of change and transformation in individuals, communities, and societies.

Importance, Uses, and Interdependence

Importance, Uses, and Interdependence in Integral Theory

Integral Theory, a comprehensive framework developed by philosopher Ken Wilber, holds significant importance in various fields due to its versatility, holistic approach, and emphasis on interconnectedness. By understanding the importance, uses, and interdependence inherent in Integral Theory, individuals and organizations can gain valuable insights and navigate complex challenges more effectively.

One of the key aspects of Integral Theory's importance lies in its holistic approach to understanding reality. By incorporating multiple dimensions and perspectives, Integral Theory offers a comprehensive framework for analyzing complex phenomena. This holistic perspective is essential for addressing multifaceted challenges such as climate change, social inequality, and global health crises. Integral Theory's emphasis on interconnectedness underscores the interdependence of all phenomena, highlighting the need for integrated approaches to problem-solving and decision-making.

Integral Theory finds uses across various disciplines and fields, including psychology, sociology, business, education, and spirituality. In psychology, Integral Theory provides a comprehensive framework for understanding human behavior and mental processes. By integrating insights from various psychological perspectives, researchers and practitioners can develop more effective interventions and treatments. In sociology, Integral Theory offers insights into the dynamics of social systems and cultural evolution, informing efforts to address social inequality and promote social justice. In business, Integral Theory emphasizes the importance of considering multiple stakeholders and balancing competing interests to achieve sustainable and ethical outcomes. In education, Integral Theory advocates for a holistic approach to learning that addresses the cognitive, emotional, and spiritual dimensions of education. In spirituality, Integral Theory offers a framework for integrating different religious and mystical traditions, recognizing the validity of diverse spiritual experiences and practices.

Integral Theory also highlights the interdependence of different dimensions and perspectives. Integral Theory's emphasis on quadrants, levels, lines, and states underscores the interconnectedness of individual and collective, interior and exterior dimensions. For example, changes in individual consciousness (quadrant I) may lead to shifts in social norms and cultural practices (quadrant III), which in turn may influence the structures and institutions of society (quadrant IV). By considering these interrelations, Integral Theory offers insights into the dynamics of change and transformation at both the individual and collective levels.

Moreover, Integral Theory's emphasis on interdependence has practical implications for personal and societal transformation. By recognizing the interconnectedness of all phenomena, individuals and organizations can develop more holistic approaches to problem-solving and decision-making. Integral Theory's holistic perspective encourages collaboration, empathy, and compassion, fostering positive change at both the individual and collective levels.

In conclusion, Integral Theory holds significant importance due to its holistic approach, versatility, and emphasis on interconnectedness. By understanding the importance, uses, and interdependence inherent in Integral Theory, individuals and organizations can gain valuable insights and navigate complex challenges more effectively. Integral Theory's comprehensive framework offers a roadmap for personal and societal transformation, highlighting the interconnectedness of all phenomena and the importance of integrated approaches to problem-solving and decision-making. As individuals and organizations continue to grapple with the complexities of the modern world, Integral Theory remains a valuable tool for fostering understanding, empathy, and positive change.

Examples and Case Studies of Quadrants

Examples and Case Studies of Quadrants in Integral Theory

Integral Theory, developed by philosopher Ken Wilber, introduces the concept of quadrants as a fundamental aspect of understanding reality. These quadrants offer a multidimensional lens through which complex phenomena can be analyzed, providing insights into the interconnected nature of individual and collective existence. Let's explore some examples and case studies that illustrate the application of quadrants in Integral Theory.

One example of quadrants in action can be seen in the study of mental health and well-being. In the first quadrant (individual interior), psychologists may explore the subjective experiences and consciousness of individuals, including their thoughts, emotions, and beliefs. Through methods such as psychotherapy and introspection, researchers gain insight into the inner workings of the mind and the psychological factors that contribute to mental health issues such as depression and anxiety.

In the second quadrant (individual exterior), researchers may examine the observable behaviors and physiological processes associated with mental health. This could include studying brain activity using neuroimaging techniques, analyzing hormonal levels, or observing behavioral patterns. By understanding the external manifestations of mental health issues, researchers can develop more effective interventions and treatments.

Moving to the third quadrant (collective interior), sociologists and anthropologists may explore the cultural and social dimensions of mental health. This could involve studying cultural beliefs and attitudes towards mental illness, as well as the impact of social norms and stigma on individuals' experiences. By understanding the cultural context of mental health, researchers can develop culturally sensitive interventions and promote social support and acceptance.

Finally, in the fourth quadrant (collective exterior), researchers may examine the structural and systemic factors that influence mental health at the societal level. This could include analyzing access to healthcare services, socioeconomic disparities, and policies related to mental health care. By addressing systemic barriers and inequalities, policymakers can create environments that support mental well-being for all members of society.

Another example of quadrants in action can be seen in the study of environmental sustainability. In the first quadrant (individual interior), environmental psychologists may explore individuals' attitudes, values, and beliefs towards nature and the environment. By understanding the psychological factors that influence pro-environmental behaviors, researchers can develop interventions to promote sustainable behaviors such as recycling and conservation.

In the second quadrant (individual exterior), researchers may examine the observable impacts of human activities on the environment, such as deforestation, pollution, and climate change. This could involve collecting data on carbon emissions, habitat loss, and biodiversity decline. By understanding the external consequences of human actions, policymakers can develop policies and regulations to mitigate environmental degradation.

In the third quadrant (collective interior), researchers may explore the cultural and social dimensions of environmental sustainability. This could include studying cultural values and worldviews that shape attitudes towards nature, as well as the role of social norms and collective action in promoting environmental conservation. By fostering a culture of sustainability, communities can work together to address environmental challenges and protect natural resources.

Finally, in the fourth quadrant (collective exterior), researchers may examine the structural and systemic factors that influence environmental sustainability at the societal level. This could include analyzing government policies, corporate practices, and international agreements related to environmental protection. By advocating for systemic change and promoting sustainable development practices, policymakers can create a more resilient and equitable future for both people and the planet.

In conclusion, examples and case studies of quadrants in Integral Theory illustrate how this multidimensional framework can be applied to analyze complex phenomena and address real-world challenges. By considering the individual and collective, interior and exterior dimensions, researchers can gain a more comprehensive understanding of the interconnectedness of all phenomena. This holistic approach allows for a deeper analysis of complex issues and provides insights into effective strategies for positive change. As individuals and organizations continue to grapple with the complexities of the modern world, Integral Theory remains a valuable tool for fostering understanding, empathy, and sustainable solutions.

Levels and Lines in Integral Theory

Levels and Lines in Integral Theory

Integral Theory, developed by philosopher Ken Wilber, introduces the concepts of levels and lines as fundamental aspects of understanding human development and consciousness. These concepts offer a nuanced perspective on the multidimensional nature of growth and evolution, providing insights into the diverse paths individuals may traverse throughout their lives.

Levels, in Integral Theory, refer to the stages of development that individuals, cultures, and societies progress through over time. These stages represent increasingly complex ways of organizing and understanding the world, with each level building upon and transcending the previous one. Integral Theory identifies several levels of development, including but not limited to:

Archaic: The earliest stage of development, characterized by basic survival instincts and reflexive behavior.
Magical: The emergence of magical thinking and animistic beliefs, often associated with early childhood.
Mythic: The development of mythic and religious beliefs, characterized by a strong emphasis on tradition, authority, and morality.
Rational: The emergence of rational and scientific thinking, marked by an emphasis on logic, reason, and empirical evidence.
Integral: The highest stage of development, characterized by an ability to integrate multiple perspectives and transcend polarities.
Lines, on the other hand, refer to the different aspects of human potential that can be developed over time. These lines represent various domains of growth and mastery, such as cognitive intelligence, emotional intelligence, moral development, and aesthetic sensitivity. Integral Theory identifies multiple lines of development, each of which may progress independently and at different rates. Some examples of lines of development include:

Cognitive: The development of cognitive abilities such as problem-solving, critical thinking, and abstract reasoning.
Emotional: The development of emotional intelligence, including self-awareness, empathy, and emotional regulation.
Moral: The development of moral reasoning and ethical decision-making, including principles such as fairness, justice, and compassion.

Interpersonal: The development of social skills and interpersonal relationships, including communication, conflict resolution, and collaboration.
Integral Theory emphasizes the interplay between levels and lines of development, recognizing that individuals may progress through different stages of growth in each domain. For example, someone may exhibit advanced cognitive abilities (e.g., rational thinking) while still struggling with emotional regulation (e.g., emotional reactivity). Similarly, cultures and societies may exhibit varying levels of development across different domains, leading to complex interactions and dynamics.

Understanding levels and lines in Integral Theory offers valuable insights into personal growth and development, as well as societal change and transformation. By recognizing the multidimensional nature of human potential, individuals and organizations can cultivate a more holistic approach to personal and collective evolution. This awareness allows for greater self-awareness, empathy, and understanding, fostering positive change at both the individual and societal levels.

Moreover, Integral Theory's emphasis on levels and lines of development has practical implications for education, psychology, leadership, and organizational development. By recognizing the diversity of human potential and the importance of addressing multiple domains of growth, educators can design more effective learning experiences that meet the needs of all learners. Similarly, psychologists and therapists can tailor interventions to target specific areas of development, leading to more personalized and impactful outcomes.

In conclusion, levels and lines in Integral Theory provide a comprehensive framework for understanding human development and consciousness. By recognizing the multidimensional nature of growth and evolution, individuals and organizations can cultivate a more holistic approach to personal and collective transformation. This awareness offers valuable insights into personal growth, societal change, and the interconnectedness of all phenomena. As individuals and societies continue to navigate the complexities of the modern world, Integral Theory remains a valuable tool for fostering understanding, empathy, and positive change.

Exploring Different Levels

Exploring Different Levels in Integral Theory

Integral Theory, developed by philosopher Ken Wilber, offers a profound perspective on human development and consciousness, emphasizing the existence of different levels through which individuals, cultures, and societies progress over time. These levels represent increasingly complex stages of growth and evolution, each building upon and transcending the previous one. Let's delve into the exploration of different levels in Integral Theory to gain a deeper understanding of this fascinating concept.

At the foundational level of development in Integral Theory lies the archaic stage. This level is characterized by basic survival instincts and reflexive behavior. Individuals at this stage operate primarily on instinctual impulses, responding to immediate needs for food, shelter, and safety. While this level may seem primitive compared to higher stages of development, it forms the essential groundwork upon which more complex levels are built.

Moving beyond the archaic stage, we encounter the magical stage of development. Here, individuals begin to develop magical thinking and animistic beliefs, often associated with early childhood. Magical thought patterns involve a belief in supernatural forces and a sense of connection with the natural world. This stage is characterized by a rich imagination and a belief in the power of symbols and rituals to influence the world around them.

The next stage of development in Integral Theory is the mythic stage. At this level, individuals embrace mythic and religious beliefs, often characterized by a strong emphasis on tradition, authority, and morality. Myths and religious stories provide a framework for understanding the world and one's place within it. This stage is marked by a sense of belonging to a larger community and a commitment to upholding shared values and beliefs.

As individuals progress through the mythic stage, they enter the rational stage of development. Here, individuals begin to embrace rational and scientific thinking, marked by an emphasis on logic, reason, and empirical evidence. This stage represents a significant shift from reliance on tradition and authority to critical thinking and independent inquiry. Rational thought allows individuals to question existing beliefs and explore new ideas, leading to advances in science, technology, and philosophy.

Finally, at the pinnacle of development in Integral Theory lies the integral stage. This stage represents the highest level of development, characterized by an ability to integrate multiple perspectives and transcend polarities. Individuals at this stage possess a deep awareness of the interconnectedness of all phenomena and a sense of unity with the universe. Integral thinkers are able to navigate complexity with ease, recognizing the inherent contradictions and paradoxes of existence.

Integral Theory emphasizes the importance of recognizing and embracing the diversity of levels of development within individuals and societies. Each level offers valuable insights and perspectives, contributing to the richness and complexity of human experience. By understanding the different levels of development, individuals can cultivate greater self-awareness, empathy, and understanding of others.

Moreover, Integral Theory suggests that individuals and societies may progress through these levels at different rates and in different domains. While someone may exhibit advanced cognitive abilities (e.g., rational thinking), they may still struggle with emotional regulation (e.g., emotional reactivity). Similarly, cultures and societies may exhibit varying levels of development across different domains, leading to complex interactions and dynamics.

In conclusion, exploring different levels in Integral Theory offers valuable insights into human development and consciousness. By recognizing the diversity of levels within individuals and societies, we can cultivate a deeper understanding of ourselves and others. This awareness fosters empathy, compassion, and a sense of interconnectedness, ultimately contributing to personal growth and collective evolution. As individuals and societies continue to navigate the complexities of the modern world, Integral Theory remains a valuable framework for fostering understanding, empathy, and positive change.

Understanding the Lines

Understanding the Lines in Integral Theory

Integral Theory, developed by philosopher Ken Wilber, offers a comprehensive framework for understanding human development and consciousness. Central to this framework are the concepts of lines, which represent different aspects of human potential that can be developed over time. These lines provide insight into the diverse domains of growth and mastery that individuals may traverse throughout their lives. Let's explore the significance of understanding the lines in Integral Theory and how they contribute to a deeper understanding of human potential.

In Integral Theory, lines refer to various dimensions of human development, each representing a distinct aspect of human potential. These lines include cognitive, emotional, moral, interpersonal, and spiritual dimensions, among others. By recognizing the diversity of lines, Integral Theory offers a holistic perspective on human development, emphasizing the importance of addressing multiple domains of growth.

One of the most well-known lines in Integral Theory is the cognitive line. This line represents the development of cognitive abilities such as problem-solving, critical thinking, and abstract reasoning. Individuals progress through different stages of cognitive development, from simple sensory-motor responses in infancy to complex abstract reasoning in adulthood. By understanding the cognitive line, educators, psychologists, and policymakers can design more effective learning experiences and interventions that meet the needs of learners at different stages of development.

Another important line in Integral Theory is the emotional line. This line represents the development of emotional intelligence, including self-awareness, empathy, and emotional regulation. Individuals progress through different stages of emotional development, from basic emotional responses in infancy to nuanced emotional understanding and empathy in adulthood. By understanding the emotional line, therapists, educators, and leaders can cultivate environments that support emotional well-being and resilience.

Integral Theory also emphasizes the moral line, which represents the development of moral reasoning and ethical decision-making. This line encompasses principles such as fairness, justice, and compassion, as individuals progress from egocentric to ethnocentric to world-centric moral orientations. By understanding the moral line, educators, policymakers, and leaders can promote ethical behavior and social responsibility in individuals and communities.

The interpersonal line is another important aspect of human development in Integral Theory. This line represents the development of social skills and interpersonal relationships, including communication, cooperation, and conflict resolution. Individuals progress from basic social interactions in infancy to complex social networks and relationships in adulthood. By understanding the interpersonal line, educators, therapists, and organizational leaders can foster positive social connections and teamwork.

Integral Theory also recognizes the importance of the spiritual line, which represents the development of spiritual awareness and insight. This line encompasses experiences of connection, meaning, and purpose, as individuals progress from egocentric to ethnocentric to world-centric spiritual perspectives. By understanding the spiritual line, individuals can cultivate a deeper sense of meaning and purpose in their lives, leading to greater fulfillment and well-being.

In conclusion, understanding the lines in Integral Theory offers valuable insights into human development and consciousness. By recognizing the diversity of lines, Integral Theory provides a holistic perspective on human potential, emphasizing the importance of addressing multiple dimensions of growth. This awareness fosters personal growth, social development, and spiritual awakening, ultimately contributing to a more compassionate, resilient, and interconnected world. As individuals and societies continue to navigate the complexities of the modern world, Integral Theory remains a valuable framework for fostering understanding, empathy, and positive change.

Interplay between Levels and Lines

The Interplay between Levels and Lines in Integral Theory

Integral Theory, developed by philosopher Ken Wilber, offers a comprehensive framework for understanding human development and consciousness. Central to this framework is the interplay between levels and lines, which provides insight into the multidimensional nature of growth and evolution. Understanding how levels and lines interact can lead to a deeper understanding of human potential and the complexities of personal and collective transformation.

Levels, in Integral Theory, represent the stages of development that individuals, cultures, and societies progress through over time. These levels encompass a wide range of domains, including cognitive, emotional, moral, interpersonal, and spiritual dimensions. Each level represents a more complex way of organizing and understanding the world, building upon and transcending the previous one. Individuals progress through these levels as they mature and evolve, gaining new insights and capabilities along the way.

Lines, on the other hand, represent different aspects of human potential that can be developed over time. These lines encompass various domains of growth and mastery, such as cognitive intelligence, emotional intelligence, moral development, and interpersonal skills. Each line progresses independently and at different rates, allowing individuals to excel in certain areas while still developing in others.

The interplay between levels and lines in Integral Theory highlights the dynamic and interconnected nature of human development. Individuals progress through different stages of growth in each domain, with the development of one line influencing and shaping the development of others. For example, someone may exhibit advanced cognitive abilities (e.g., rational thinking) while still struggling with emotional regulation (e.g., emotional reactivity). Similarly, cultures and societies may exhibit varying levels of development across different domains, leading to complex interactions and dynamics.

Moreover, Integral Theory suggests that the interplay between levels and lines can lead to emergent properties and dynamics. As individuals progress through higher levels of development, they may exhibit new capacities and abilities that were not present at lower levels. For example, someone at a higher level of moral development may exhibit greater empathy and compassion towards others, leading to more ethical behavior and decision-making.

Similarly, as cultures and societies progress through higher levels of development, they may exhibit new forms of social organization and cultural expression. For example, societies at higher levels of development may prioritize social justice and environmental sustainability, leading to more equitable and environmentally conscious policies and practices.

Understanding the interplay between levels and lines in Integral Theory offers valuable insights into personal growth and societal change. By recognizing the multidimensional nature of human potential, individuals and organizations can cultivate a more holistic approach to personal and collective transformation. This awareness fosters empathy, understanding, and collaboration, ultimately contributing to a more compassionate, resilient, and interconnected world.

In conclusion, the interplay between levels and lines in Integral Theory highlights the dynamic and interconnected nature of human development. By recognizing the multidimensional nature of human potential, individuals and organizations can cultivate a more holistic approach to personal and collective transformation. This awareness fosters empathy, understanding, and collaboration, ultimately contributing to a more compassionate, resilient, and interconnected world. As individuals and societies continue to navigate the complexities of the modern world, Integral Theory remains a valuable framework for fostering understanding, empathy, and positive change.

States and Types in Integral Theory

States and Types in Integral Theory

Integral Theory, developed by philosopher Ken Wilber, offers a rich and multifaceted framework for understanding human consciousness and development. Central to this framework are the concepts of states and types, which provide insight into the diverse dimensions of human experience and expression. Understanding states and types in Integral Theory can deepen our understanding of the complexity of human consciousness and behavior.

States, in Integral Theory, refer to different states of consciousness that individuals may experience at various times. These states can range from ordinary waking consciousness to extraordinary states of consciousness such as meditation, flow, or mystical experiences. Integral Theory recognizes that individuals can access different states of consciousness through various practices such as meditation, prayer, psychedelics, or intense physical activity.

States of consciousness are characterized by their subjective qualities, including perceptions, emotions, and cognitive processes. For example, a meditative state may be characterized by feelings of inner peace, clarity of mind, and a sense of connection with the universe. In contrast, a state of anxiety may be characterized by feelings of fear, restlessness, and cognitive distortions.

Integral Theory emphasizes the importance of recognizing and integrating different states of consciousness into our lives. By accessing and exploring different states of consciousness, individuals can gain new insights, perspectives, and ways of being in the world. This can lead to personal growth, creativity, and spiritual awakening.

Types, on the other hand, refer to different personality traits, characteristics, or typologies that individuals may possess. Integral Theory recognizes that individuals have unique combinations of personality traits that shape their behavior, preferences, and interactions with others. These types can include personality traits such as introversion/extroversion, openness, conscientiousness, agreeableness, and neuroticism, among others.

Types of personality are characterized by their enduring patterns of behavior, thoughts, and feelings across different situations. For example, an individual who is high in openness may be curious, imaginative, and open to new experiences, while someone who is high in conscientiousness may be organized, responsible, and disciplined in their behavior.

Integral Theory emphasizes the importance of understanding and honoring the diversity of personality types within individuals and groups. By recognizing and appreciating different personality traits, individuals can cultivate empathy, understanding, and collaboration in their interactions with others. This can lead to healthier relationships, more effective teamwork, and greater social cohesion.

Moreover, Integral Theory suggests that individuals may develop and integrate different states and types of consciousness over time. For example, someone who practices meditation regularly may cultivate a more stable and integrated state of inner peace and mindfulness. Similarly, someone who engages in personal development work may develop greater self-awareness and emotional intelligence, leading to a more balanced and harmonious personality.

Understanding states and types in Integral Theory offers valuable insights into the complexity of human consciousness and behavior. By recognizing the diversity of states of consciousness and personality types, individuals can cultivate a deeper understanding of themselves and others. This awareness fosters personal growth, interpersonal relationships, and social harmony, ultimately contributing to a more compassionate, resilient, and interconnected world.

In conclusion, states and types in Integral Theory provide a comprehensive framework for understanding human consciousness and behavior. By recognizing and integrating different states of consciousness and personality types, individuals can cultivate a deeper understanding of themselves and others. This awareness fosters personal growth, interpersonal relationships, and social harmony, ultimately contributing to a more compassionate, resilient, and interconnected world. As individuals and societies continue to navigate the complexities of the modern world, Integral Theory remains a valuable framework for fostering understanding, empathy, and positive change.

Characteristics & Importance of States

Characteristics & Importance of States in Integral Theory

States of consciousness play a pivotal role in Integral Theory, a comprehensive framework developed by philosopher Ken Wilber. These states represent different modes of awareness and experience that individuals may encounter throughout their lives. Understanding the characteristics and importance of states in Integral Theory can deepen our comprehension of human consciousness and personal development.

One key characteristic of states in Integral Theory is their transient nature. States of consciousness are not permanent traits but rather temporary states that individuals can access through various practices such as meditation, prayer, or intense physical activity. These states can range from ordinary waking consciousness to extraordinary states such as meditation, flow, or mystical experiences. Integral Theory recognizes that individuals can move in and out of different states of consciousness depending on their circumstances and practices.

Another characteristic of states in Integral Theory is their subjective qualities. Each state of consciousness is characterized by its unique perceptions, emotions, and cognitive processes. For example, a meditative state may be characterized by feelings of inner peace, clarity of mind, and a sense of unity with the universe. In contrast, a state of anxiety may be characterized by feelings of fear, restlessness, and cognitive distortions.

Integral Theory emphasizes the importance of recognizing and integrating different states of consciousness into our lives. By accessing and exploring different states of consciousness, individuals can gain new insights, perspectives, and ways of being in the world. This can lead to personal growth, creativity, and spiritual awakening. Additionally, integrating different states of consciousness can lead to a more balanced and harmonious life, allowing individuals to navigate challenges with greater resilience and clarity.

Furthermore, states of consciousness can have profound effects on individuals' behavior, perceptions, and relationships. For example, individuals who regularly practice meditation may cultivate greater self-awareness, emotional intelligence, and compassion towards others. Similarly, individuals who experience flow states during creative or athletic activities may feel more engaged, focused, and fulfilled in their pursuits. By cultivating positive states of consciousness, individuals can enhance their overall well-being and quality of life.

The importance of states in Integral Theory extends beyond individual well-being to societal and cultural transformation. Integral Theory recognizes that collective states of consciousness can influence the values, beliefs, and behaviors of entire communities and societies. For example, societies that cultivate states of compassion, empathy, and cooperation may exhibit greater social cohesion and resilience in the face of challenges. Conversely, societies that are dominated by states of fear, aggression, and division may experience conflict, injustice, and inequality.

Understanding the importance of states in Integral Theory can inform personal growth, interpersonal relationships, and societal change. By recognizing the transient nature and subjective qualities of states of consciousness, individuals can cultivate a deeper understanding of themselves and others. This awareness fosters empathy, compassion, and resilience, ultimately contributing to a more harmonious and interconnected world.

In conclusion, states of consciousness are central to Integral Theory, offering valuable insights into human consciousness and personal development. By recognizing the characteristics and importance of states, individuals can cultivate a deeper understanding of themselves and others. This awareness fosters personal growth, interpersonal relationships, and societal change, ultimately contributing to a more compassionate, resilient, and interconnected world. As individuals and societies continue to navigate the complexities of the modern world, Integral Theory remains a valuable framework for fostering understanding, empathy, and positive change.

Understanding Different Types

Understanding Different Types in Integral Theory

Integral Theory, developed by philosopher Ken Wilber, offers a comprehensive framework for understanding human consciousness and development. A central aspect of this framework is the concept of different types, which refers to the various personality traits, characteristics, or typologies that individuals may possess. Understanding the different types in Integral Theory can provide valuable insights into the diversity and complexity of human behavior.

One key characteristic of different types in Integral Theory is their diversity. Integral Theory recognizes that individuals have unique combinations of personality traits that shape their behavior, preferences, and interactions with others. These types can encompass a wide range of dimensions, including introversion/extroversion, openness, conscientiousness, agreeableness, and neuroticism, among others.

Each type is characterized by its enduring patterns of behavior, thoughts, and feelings across different situations. For example, an individual who is high in introversion may prefer solitary activities and recharge by spending time alone, while someone who is high in extraversion may thrive in social settings and gain energy from interacting with others.

Another characteristic of different types in Integral Theory is their influence on individuals' behavior and decision-making. Integral Theory recognizes that personality traits play a significant role in shaping how individuals perceive and respond to their environment. For example, someone who is high in openness may be more willing to try new experiences and explore unfamiliar ideas, while someone who is high in conscientiousness may be more organized and disciplined in their approach to tasks and responsibilities.

Integral Theory emphasizes the importance of understanding and honoring the diversity of personality types within individuals and groups. By recognizing and appreciating different personality traits, individuals can cultivate empathy, understanding, and collaboration in their interactions with others. This can lead to healthier relationships, more effective teamwork, and greater social cohesion.

Moreover, Integral Theory suggests that individuals may develop and integrate different types of personality traits over time. For example, someone who engages in personal development work may develop greater self-awareness and emotional intelligence, leading to a more balanced and harmonious personality. Similarly, individuals may adapt their behavior and preferences in response to changing circumstances and life experiences.

Understanding the different types in Integral Theory can also have practical implications for personal growth and development. By recognizing their own personality traits and tendencies, individuals can gain insight into their strengths and areas for growth. This self-awareness can inform personal goals, decision-making, and interpersonal relationships, leading to greater fulfillment and well-being.

Additionally, understanding the different types in Integral Theory can inform leadership and organizational development. By recognizing the diversity of personality traits within teams and organizations, leaders can create environments that support individuals' strengths and preferences. This can lead to more effective communication, collaboration, and innovation, ultimately contributing to organizational success.

In conclusion, understanding different types in Integral Theory offers valuable insights into the diversity and complexity of human behavior. By recognizing and appreciating the unique combinations of personality traits within individuals, we can cultivate empathy, understanding, and collaboration in our interactions with others. This awareness fosters personal growth, interpersonal relationships, and organizational success, ultimately contributing to a more harmonious and interconnected world. As individuals and societies continue to navigate the complexities of the modern world, Integral Theory remains a valuable framework for fostering understanding, empathy, and positive change.

Connection between States and Types

The Connection between States and Types in Integral Theory

Integral Theory, founded by philosopher Ken Wilber, provides a holistic framework for understanding human consciousness and development. At the heart of this framework lies the intricate connection between states and types, two fundamental aspects of human experience. Understanding the relationship between states and types in Integral Theory offers profound insights into the complexity of human consciousness and behavior.

States of consciousness, as discussed in Integral Theory, refer to different modes of awareness and experience that individuals may access. These states can range from ordinary waking consciousness to extraordinary experiences such as meditation, flow, or mystical states. On the other hand, types in Integral Theory represent various personality traits, characteristics, or typologies that individuals may possess, influencing their behavior, preferences, and interactions with others.

The connection between states and types lies in their reciprocal influence on each other. States of consciousness can shape and influence the expression of personality traits, while personality traits can also influence the states of consciousness that individuals access. For example, an individual who is naturally more open-minded and curious (a personality trait) may be more inclined to explore altered states of consciousness through practices such as meditation or psychedelic experiences. Similarly, someone who is naturally more anxious or neurotic may find it challenging to access states of relaxation or inner peace.

Conversely, the states of consciousness that individuals access can also influence the expression of personality traits. For example, someone who regularly experiences states of mindfulness and equanimity through meditation practice may develop greater emotional resilience and self-awareness, leading to shifts in their personality traits over time. Similarly, individuals who experience states of flow during creative or athletic activities may develop a sense of mastery and confidence that influences their behavior and preferences.

Integral Theory emphasizes the importance of recognizing and integrating both states and types into our understanding of human consciousness and behavior. By recognizing the reciprocal influence between states and types, we can cultivate a deeper understanding of ourselves and others. This awareness fosters empathy, compassion, and personal growth, ultimately contributing to a more harmonious and interconnected world.

Moreover, understanding the connection between states and types can have practical implications for personal development and well-being. By recognizing how different states of consciousness can influence our behavior and personality traits, we can cultivate practices that support positive states of mind and emotional resilience. Similarly, by recognizing how our personality traits may influence the states of consciousness we access, we can cultivate self-awareness and choose practices that support our growth and development.

Additionally, understanding the connection between states and types can inform therapeutic interventions and approaches. By recognizing how certain states of consciousness may be linked to specific personality traits or psychological issues, therapists can tailor interventions to address the underlying causes of distress and support clients in accessing more positive states of mind. Similarly, by recognizing how personality traits may influence the states of consciousness that individuals access, therapists can help clients develop strategies for managing their emotions and cultivating greater well-being.

In conclusion, the connection between states and types in Integral Theory offers valuable insights into the complexity of human consciousness and behavior. By recognizing the reciprocal influence between states of consciousness and personality traits, we can cultivate a deeper understanding of ourselves and others. This awareness fosters personal growth, interpersonal relationships, and well-being, ultimately contributing to a more harmonious and interconnected world. As individuals and societies continue to navigate the complexities of the modern world, Integral Theory remains a valuable framework for fostering understanding, empathy, and positive change.

Integral Life Practice

Integral Life Practice: Cultivating Holistic Well-being

Integral Life Practice (ILP) is a transformative approach to personal development and well-being rooted in Integral Theory, a comprehensive framework developed by philosopher Ken Wilber. ILP integrates various practices from different domains of human experience, including body, mind, spirit, and relationships, into a cohesive and comprehensive approach to personal growth.

At its core, ILP recognizes that human beings are multifaceted and multidimensional beings, with physical, emotional, mental, and spiritual aspects that are interconnected and interdependent. Therefore, to achieve holistic well-being, it is essential to address and integrate all dimensions of our being. ILP provides a structured framework for doing so, offering a roadmap for personal growth and transformation.

One of the key components of Integral Life Practice is physical practice, which focuses on cultivating health, vitality, and embodiment. This may include practices such as yoga, qigong, martial arts, or physical exercise, all of which promote physical fitness, flexibility, and resilience. Physical practice not only enhances physical health but also helps to cultivate presence and awareness in the body, fostering a deeper connection between body, mind, and spirit.

Another essential component of ILP is cognitive practice, which involves the cultivation of mental clarity, focus, and discernment. This may include practices such as meditation, mindfulness, or cognitive exercises designed to enhance cognitive function and emotional regulation. Cognitive practice helps to cultivate inner peace, clarity of mind, and emotional resilience, enabling individuals to navigate the complexities of life with greater ease and grace.

Spiritual practice is also integral to ILP, encompassing practices that cultivate a deeper connection with the transcendent or divine aspects of existence. This may include practices such as prayer, contemplation, or rituals that facilitate spiritual growth and awakening. Spiritual practice helps individuals to connect with a sense of meaning, purpose, and interconnectedness, fostering a sense of inner peace and fulfillment.

Furthermore, ILP emphasizes the importance of relational practice, which involves cultivating healthy and fulfilling relationships with others. This may include practices such as communication skills, conflict resolution, or empathy training, all of which promote compassionate and authentic relating. Relational practice helps individuals to cultivate empathy, understanding, and connection with others, fostering deeper and more meaningful relationships.

Integral Life Practice encourages individuals to integrate these practices into their daily lives in a balanced and sustainable way, recognizing that each dimension of practice contributes to overall well-being. By engaging in physical, cognitive, spiritual, and relational practices regularly, individuals can cultivate greater health, happiness, and fulfillment in all areas of their lives.

Moreover, ILP recognizes that personal growth and transformation are ongoing processes that unfold over time. Therefore, ILP emphasizes the importance of self-reflection, self-awareness, and ongoing learning as essential aspects of the practice. By continuously exploring and evolving our understanding of ourselves and the world around us, we can deepen our practice and cultivate greater wisdom and insight.

In conclusion, Integral Life Practice offers a transformative approach to personal development and well-being, rooted in Integral Theory. By integrating practices from different domains of human experience, including body, mind, spirit, and relationships, ILP provides a comprehensive framework for cultivating holistic well-being. By engaging in physical, cognitive, spiritual, and relational practices regularly, individuals can cultivate greater health, happiness, and fulfillment in all areas of their lives. As individuals and societies continue to navigate the complexities of the modern world, Integral Life Practice remains a valuable tool for fostering personal growth, resilience, and flourishing.

Introduction to Integral Life Practice

Integral Life Practice: A Holistic Approach to Personal Growth

Integral Life Practice (ILP) stands as a transformative methodology within the realm of personal development, deeply rooted in the comprehensive framework of Integral Theory. Conceived by philosopher Ken Wilber, Integral Theory provides a holistic understanding of human consciousness and development, emphasizing the integration of various aspects of our being. Integral Life Practice takes this philosophy a step further, offering a structured approach to personal growth that encompasses body, mind, spirit, and relationships.

At its core, ILP recognizes the multi-faceted nature of human existence, acknowledging that individuals are comprised of physical, emotional, mental, and spiritual dimensions. By addressing each of these dimensions through intentional practices, ILP aims to cultivate holistic well-being and facilitate personal transformation.

One of the fundamental pillars of Integral Life Practice is physical practice. This component focuses on nurturing health, vitality, and embodiment. Through practices such as yoga, tai chi, or physical exercise, individuals can enhance their physical fitness, flexibility, and resilience. Physical practice not only strengthens the body but also fosters a deeper connection between body, mind, and spirit, promoting overall wellness and vitality.

Closely intertwined with physical practice is cognitive practice, which emphasizes the cultivation of mental clarity, focus, and discernment. Meditation, mindfulness, and cognitive exercises are just a few examples of practices that fall under this category. Cognitive practice helps individuals develop inner peace, emotional resilience, and heightened awareness, empowering them to navigate life's challenges with greater ease and presence of mind.

Spiritual practice is another integral component of ILP, focusing on nurturing a deeper connection with the transcendent or divine aspects of existence. Through practices such as prayer, meditation, or contemplation, individuals can explore their spiritual nature and cultivate a sense of meaning, purpose, and interconnectedness. Spiritual practice offers a pathway to inner peace, fulfillment, and spiritual awakening.

Relational practice rounds out the spectrum of Integral Life Practice, emphasizing the importance of cultivating healthy and authentic relationships with others. Communication skills, empathy training, and conflict resolution techniques are examples of practices that fall under this category. Relational practice fosters empathy, understanding, and connection, enriching interpersonal relationships and promoting social harmony.

Integral Life Practice encourages individuals to integrate these practices into their daily lives in a balanced and sustainable manner. By engaging in physical, cognitive, spiritual, and relational practices regularly, individuals can cultivate greater health, happiness, and fulfillment across all dimensions of their lives.

Furthermore, ILP recognizes that personal growth and transformation are ongoing processes that require self-reflection, self-awareness, and continual learning. By cultivating a mindset of curiosity, openness, and exploration, individuals can deepen their practice and evolve their understanding of themselves and the world around them.

In conclusion, Integral Life Practice offers a holistic and transformative approach to personal growth, rooted in the comprehensive framework of Integral Theory. By integrating practices from different domains of human experience, ILP provides a structured pathway to holistic well-being and personal transformation. As individuals continue on their journey of self-discovery and growth, Integral Life Practice serves as a guiding light, empowering them to cultivate health, happiness, and fulfillment in all aspects of their lives.

Its Role in Integral Theory

Integral Theory has emerged as a groundbreaking framework for understanding human consciousness and development. At the heart of this theory lies a concept that serves as a unifying force, guiding its principles and applications: Integral Life Practice (ILP). ILP plays a crucial role in Integral Theory, serving as a practical methodology for individuals to embody the theory's principles and cultivate holistic well-being across all dimensions of their lives.

Integral Theory, developed by philosopher Ken Wilber, encompasses a broad range of concepts and perspectives, integrating various disciplines such as psychology, spirituality, sociology, and philosophy. It posits that human beings are multi-dimensional beings, consisting of physical, emotional, mental, and spiritual dimensions, all of which are interconnected and interdependent. ILP serves as a bridge between theory and practice, offering a structured approach for individuals to apply Integral Theory's principles to their daily lives.

One of the key roles of ILP in Integral Theory is to provide a comprehensive framework for personal growth and development. By integrating practices from different domains of human experience – including physical, cognitive, spiritual, and relational practices – ILP offers individuals a holistic pathway to self-transformation. Through engaging in these practices, individuals can cultivate greater health, happiness, and fulfillment in all aspects of their lives.

Moreover, ILP serves as a practical tool for embodying the core principles of Integral Theory. Integral Theory emphasizes the importance of recognizing and honoring the diversity and interconnectedness of human experience. ILP encourages individuals to integrate practices from different dimensions of human experience, fostering a deeper understanding of the integral nature of reality and promoting harmony and balance across all aspects of life.

Another important role of ILP in Integral Theory is to foster personal and collective evolution. Integral Theory suggests that human consciousness evolves through stages of development, from egocentric to ethnocentric to world-centric perspectives. ILP provides individuals with practices that support their growth and development at each stage of consciousness, facilitating their evolution towards higher levels of awareness and integration.

Furthermore, ILP serves as a catalyst for social and cultural transformation. Integral Theory suggests that as individuals evolve and grow, so too do societies and cultures. By engaging in ILP, individuals not only cultivate their own well-being but also contribute to the evolution of collective consciousness. ILP encourages individuals to embody values such as empathy, compassion, and social responsibility, fostering positive change and creating a more harmonious and interconnected world.

In conclusion, Integral Life Practice plays a vital role in Integral Theory, serving as a practical methodology for individuals to embody the theory's principles and cultivate holistic well-being across all dimensions of their lives. By integrating practices from different domains of human experience, ILP provides individuals with a comprehensive framework for personal growth and development. Moreover, ILP fosters personal and collective evolution, serving as a catalyst for social and cultural transformation. As individuals engage in ILP, they not only cultivate their own well-being but also contribute to the evolution of consciousness and the creation of a more harmonious and interconnected world.

Step by Step Guide to Integral Life Practice

Integral Life Practice (ILP) serves as a transformative methodology within the realm of personal development, offering a structured approach to embodying the principles of Integral Theory in everyday life. As individuals seek to cultivate holistic well-being across all dimensions of their existence, ILP provides a step-by-step guide to integrating practices from different domains of human experience.

Step Assess Your Current State

The first step in embarking on an Integral Life Practice journey is to assess your current state across various dimensions of your being – physical, emotional, mental, and spiritual. Reflect on your strengths, challenges, and areas for growth in each dimension, and identify areas where you would like to focus your practice.

Step Set Intentions and Goals

Once you have assessed your current state, set clear intentions and goals for your Integral Life Practice journey. What do you hope to achieve? What areas of your life do you want to cultivate and develop? Setting intentions and goals will provide you with direction and motivation as you embark on your practice.

Step Choose Your Practices

Integral Life Practice encompasses practices from four main domains: physical, cognitive, spiritual, and relational. Choose practices from each domain that resonate with you and align with your intentions and goals. Physical practices may include yoga, tai chi, or exercise. Cognitive practices may include meditation, mindfulness, or journaling. Spiritual practices may include prayer, contemplation, or ritual. Relational practices may include communication skills, empathy training, or conflict resolution techniques.

Step Create a Daily Routine

To integrate Integral Life Practice into your daily life, create a daily routine that includes time for each of your chosen practices. Schedule dedicated time for physical, cognitive, spiritual, and relational practices, and commit to sticking to your routine consistently. Remember that consistency is key to seeing results and experiencing the benefits of your practice.

Step Practice Mindfulness and Presence

As you engage in your Integral Life Practice, cultivate mindfulness and presence in each moment. Be fully present and attentive to your experience as you engage in your practices, noticing sensations, thoughts, and emotions as they arise. Mindfulness and presence enhance the effectiveness of your practice and deepen your connection with yourself and the world around you.

Step Reflect and Adjust
Regularly reflect on your Integral Life Practice journey and evaluate your progress towards your intentions and goals. Notice what is working well and what could be improved, and be willing to adjust your practices and routines as needed. Remember that personal growth is a continuous process of learning and evolution, and be compassionate with yourself as you navigate your journey.

Step Cultivate Gratitude and Celebration
Throughout your Integral Life Practice journey, cultivate gratitude for the progress you have made and celebrate your achievements, no matter how small. Recognize the positive changes you have experienced in your life as a result of your practice, and acknowledge the effort and dedication you have invested in your personal growth and well-being.

In conclusion, Integral Life Practice offers a step-by-step guide to integrating practices from different domains of human experience into everyday life. By assessing your current state, setting intentions and goals, choosing practices, creating a daily routine, practicing mindfulness and presence, reflecting and adjusting, and cultivating gratitude and celebration, you can embark on a transformative journey of personal growth and well-being. As you engage in Integral Life Practice, remember that each step of the journey is valuable and contributes to your overall evolution as an individual.

The AQAL Framework

The AQAL Framework, standing for All Quadrants, All Levels, is a cornerstone of Integral Theory, conceived by philosopher Ken Wilber. This comprehensive framework offers a sophisticated map of reality, encompassing various dimensions of human experience and development. By incorporating multiple perspectives and dimensions, the AQAL Framework provides a holistic lens through which to understand the complexity of existence.

At the heart of the AQAL Framework are four key elements: quadrants, levels, lines, and states. These elements work together to offer a comprehensive and integrated view of reality, allowing individuals to navigate the intricacies of human consciousness and development.

The first element of the AQAL Framework is quadrants, which represent four distinct perspectives through which to understand reality: individual-interior, individual-exterior, collective-interior, and collective-exterior. The individual-interior quadrant focuses on subjective experiences such as thoughts, emotions, and beliefs. The individual-exterior quadrant encompasses objective phenomena such as behavior, biology, and the environment. The collective-interior quadrant explores shared cultural beliefs, values, and worldviews. The collective-exterior quadrant examines social systems, structures, and institutions. By considering all four quadrants, the AQAL Framework offers a more comprehensive understanding of any given phenomenon.

The second element of the AQAL Framework is levels, which represent stages of development or consciousness that individuals and societies progress through over time. These levels range from pre-personal to personal to transpersonal, encompassing various stages of cognitive, emotional, and moral development. By recognizing the existence of multiple levels of development, the AQAL Framework acknowledges the complexity and diversity of human experience.

The third element of the AQAL Framework is lines, which represent different aspects or intelligences within individuals, such as cognitive, emotional, moral, or spiritual intelligence. These lines of development can evolve independently of one another, leading to individuals who may excel in one area while lagging behind in others. By recognizing the existence of multiple lines of development, the AQAL Framework emphasizes the importance of cultivating a holistic and balanced approach to personal growth and development.

The fourth element of the AQAL Framework is states, which represent different states of consciousness that individuals may access at various times. These states can range from ordinary waking consciousness to extraordinary states such as meditation, flow, or mystical experiences. By recognizing the existence of multiple states of consciousness, the AQAL Framework highlights the fluid and dynamic nature of human experience.

Together, these four elements – quadrants, levels, lines, and states – form the AQAL Framework, providing a comprehensive and integrated map of reality. By considering multiple perspectives and dimensions, the AQAL Framework offers a more nuanced and holistic understanding of human consciousness and development. As individuals and societies continue to navigate the complexities of the modern world, the AQAL Framework remains a valuable tool for fostering understanding, empathy, and positive change.

Breaking Down the AQAL Framework

The AQAL Framework, an acronym for All Quadrants, All Levels, is a fundamental concept within Integral Theory, a comprehensive framework developed by philosopher Ken Wilber. This framework provides a holistic lens through which to understand the complexity of human consciousness and development. Breaking down the AQAL Framework reveals its intricate structure and its significance in navigating the multifaceted dimensions of reality.

At its core, the AQAL Framework comprises four essential components: quadrants, levels, lines, and states. Each of these elements contributes to a comprehensive and integrated understanding of human experience.

Quadrants represent four distinct perspectives or dimensions through which to understand reality. The individual-interior quadrant focuses on subjective experiences such as thoughts, emotions, and beliefs. The individual-exterior quadrant encompasses objective phenomena such as behavior, biology, and the environment. The collective-interior quadrant explores shared cultural beliefs, values, and worldviews. The collective-exterior quadrant examines social systems, structures, and institutions. By considering all four quadrants, the AQAL Framework provides a more complete picture of any given phenomenon.

Levels represent stages of development or consciousness that individuals and societies progress through over time. These levels range from pre-personal to personal to transpersonal, encompassing various stages of cognitive, emotional, and moral development. By recognizing the existence of multiple levels of development, the AQAL Framework acknowledges the complexity and diversity of human experience.

Lines represent different aspects or intelligences within individuals, such as cognitive, emotional, moral, or spiritual intelligence. These lines of development can evolve independently of one another, leading to individuals who may excel in one area while lagging behind in others. By recognizing the existence of multiple lines of development, the AQAL Framework emphasizes the importance of cultivating a holistic and balanced approach to personal growth and development.

States represent different states of consciousness that individuals may access at various times. These states can range from ordinary waking consciousness to extraordinary states such as meditation, flow, or mystical experiences. By recognizing the existence of multiple states of consciousness, the AQAL Framework highlights the fluid and dynamic nature of human experience.

Together, these four elements – quadrants, levels, lines, and states – form the AQAL Framework, providing a comprehensive and integrated map of reality. By considering multiple perspectives and dimensions, the AQAL Framework offers a more nuanced understanding of human consciousness and development. It serves as a valuable tool for navigating the complexities of the modern world, fostering understanding, empathy, and positive change.

In conclusion, breaking down the AQAL Framework reveals its intricate structure and its significance in understanding human consciousness and development. By incorporating multiple dimensions such as quadrants, levels, lines, and states, the AQAL Framework provides a comprehensive and integrated perspective on reality. As individuals and societies continue to navigate the complexities of the modern world, the AQAL Framework remains a valuable resource for fostering personal growth, understanding, and positive transformation.

Significance of AQAL in Integral Theory

The significance of the AQAL framework in Integral Theory cannot be overstated. It serves as the backbone of this comprehensive approach to understanding human consciousness and development, providing a sophisticated map of reality that integrates various dimensions and perspectives. Through its emphasis on All Quadrants, All Levels, the AQAL framework offers a holistic lens through which to explore the complexity of existence.

One of the key aspects of the AQAL framework is its ability to offer a comprehensive and integrated view of reality. By considering multiple dimensions such as individual and collective, subjective and objective, the AQAL framework allows for a more nuanced understanding of any given phenomenon. This holistic perspective is essential for navigating the complexities of the modern world, where issues are often multifaceted and interconnected.

Another significant aspect of the AQAL framework is its recognition of the dynamic and evolving nature of human consciousness and development. By incorporating levels of development, the AQAL framework acknowledges that individuals and societies progress through stages of growth and evolution over time. This understanding is crucial for fostering personal and collective transformation, as it provides a roadmap for navigating the complexities of human development.

Moreover, the AQAL framework emphasizes the importance of recognizing and honoring the diversity and interconnectedness of human experience. By considering multiple lines of development, such as cognitive, emotional, and spiritual intelligence, the AQAL framework highlights the richness and complexity of human potential. This recognition is essential for fostering empathy, understanding, and appreciation for the diversity of perspectives and experiences that make up the human experience.

Furthermore, the AQAL framework provides a practical tool for personal and collective growth and transformation. By offering a structured approach to understanding and navigating reality, the AQAL framework empowers individuals and communities to cultivate holistic well-being and positive change. Through practices such as Integral Life Practice, individuals can integrate the principles of the AQAL framework into their daily lives, fostering greater health, happiness, and fulfillment across all dimensions of their existence.

In addition, the AQAL framework serves as a valuable tool for addressing complex social and environmental challenges. By providing a comprehensive and integrated perspective on reality, the AQAL framework enables individuals and organizations to develop more effective strategies for addressing issues such as climate change, social inequality, and political polarization. This holistic approach is essential for fostering sustainable solutions that address the root causes of these challenges.

In conclusion, the AQAL framework holds significant importance in Integral Theory as a comprehensive and integrated approach to understanding human consciousness and development. By emphasizing All Quadrants, All Levels, the AQAL framework provides a holistic lens through which to explore the complexity of existence. Its recognition of the dynamic and evolving nature of human experience, its emphasis on diversity and interconnectedness, and its practical applications for personal and collective transformation make the AQAL framework an invaluable tool for navigating the complexities of the modern world.

Utilizing AQAL Framework in Various Fields

The AQAL Framework, standing for All Quadrants, All Levels, has found extensive application across various fields, demonstrating its versatility and efficacy as a comprehensive approach to understanding human consciousness and development. Integral Theory, pioneered by philosopher Ken Wilber, serves as the foundation for the AQAL Framework, providing a holistic lens through which to explore the complexity of reality. Utilizing the AQAL Framework in various fields has led to transformative insights and innovations, offering a new perspective on old problems and fostering holistic solutions.

In the realm of psychology and psychotherapy, the AQAL Framework has provided a valuable framework for understanding human development and addressing mental health issues. By considering multiple dimensions such as individual and collective, subjective and objective, psychologists and therapists can gain a more comprehensive understanding of their clients' experiences and tailor interventions accordingly. Moreover, the AQAL Framework's recognition of levels of development has informed therapeutic approaches that support individuals in progressing through stages of growth and evolution, fostering greater well-being and resilience.

In the field of education, the AQAL Framework has offered a holistic approach to curriculum design and pedagogy. By incorporating multiple perspectives and dimensions, educators can create learning experiences that address the diverse needs and capacities of students. Moreover, the AQAL Framework's emphasis on levels of development has informed educational practices that support students in progressing through stages of cognitive, emotional, and moral growth, fostering deeper learning and personal transformation.

In organizational development and leadership, the AQAL Framework has provided a comprehensive framework for understanding and addressing complex challenges. By considering multiple dimensions such as individual and collective, internal and external, organizations can develop more effective strategies for fostering innovation, collaboration, and resilience. Moreover, the AQAL Framework's recognition of levels of development has informed leadership practices that support individuals and teams in evolving towards higher stages of consciousness, fostering greater adaptability and agility in the face of change.

In the field of sustainability and environmental stewardship, the AQAL Framework has offered a holistic approach to addressing complex social and environmental challenges. By considering multiple perspectives and dimensions, environmentalists and activists can develop more integrated strategies for promoting ecological balance and social justice. Moreover, the AQAL Framework's emphasis on levels of development has informed sustainability practices that support individuals and communities in evolving towards more eco-conscious and regenerative ways of living.

In conclusion, the AQAL Framework has demonstrated its utility and efficacy across various fields, offering a comprehensive approach to understanding and addressing complex issues. By incorporating multiple perspectives and dimensions, the AQAL Framework provides a holistic lens through which to explore the complexity of reality and develop more integrated solutions. As individuals and societies continue to navigate the complexities of the modern world, the AQAL Framework remains a valuable tool for fostering understanding, empathy, and positive change across diverse fields of inquiry and practice.

Integral Psychology and Spirituality

Integral psychology and spirituality represent two interconnected facets of Integral Theory, a comprehensive framework developed by philosopher Ken Wilber. These components offer profound insights into the nature of human consciousness and development, emphasizing the integration of psychological and spiritual dimensions for holistic well-being.

Integral psychology delves into the depths of human consciousness, exploring the various dimensions of the psyche and their interplay with external realities. Rooted in the AQAL framework – which stands for All Quadrants, All Levels – integral psychology considers the subjective and objective, individual and collective aspects of human experience. It acknowledges that individuals are multifaceted beings, consisting of physical, emotional, mental, and spiritual dimensions, all of which interact and influence one another.

One of the central tenets of integral psychology is the recognition of multiple levels of development. These levels, ranging from pre-personal to personal to transpersonal, represent stages of cognitive, emotional, and moral growth that individuals progress through over time. Integral psychologists emphasize the importance of understanding and honoring each individual's unique developmental trajectory, recognizing that personal growth is an ongoing process that unfolds across the lifespan.

Moreover, integral psychology places a strong emphasis on shadow work – the process of exploring and integrating unconscious aspects of the psyche. By shining a light on the shadow – those parts of ourselves that we repress or deny – individuals can uncover hidden patterns and wounds that may be blocking their growth and well-being. Through practices such as therapy, meditation, and self-reflection, individuals can engage in the transformative process of shadow integration, leading to greater wholeness and authenticity.

Integral spirituality, on the other hand, explores the deeper dimensions of human experience beyond the realm of the psyche. It encompasses practices and teachings from various spiritual traditions, emphasizing the cultivation of a direct connection with the divine or transcendent aspects of existence. Integral spirituality recognizes that spirituality is a fundamental aspect of human life, intrinsic to our sense of meaning, purpose, and connection with the cosmos.

Integral spirituality emphasizes the importance of integrating spiritual insights and experiences into everyday life. Rather than relegating spirituality to isolated practices or beliefs, integral spirituality encourages individuals to embody spiritual principles in all aspects of their lives. This integration of spirituality into daily life is often referred to as integral life practice, which encompasses physical, cognitive, spiritual, and relational practices aimed at fostering holistic well-being.

Moreover, integral spirituality recognizes the importance of honoring and embracing the diversity of spiritual paths and traditions. Integral practitioners draw inspiration from a wide range of spiritual teachings and practices, recognizing that each tradition offers unique insights into the nature of reality and the human experience. By cultivating an attitude of openness, curiosity, and reverence towards different spiritual perspectives, individuals can deepen their understanding of themselves and the world around them.

In conclusion, integral psychology and spirituality offer profound insights into the nature of human consciousness and development. Rooted in the AQAL framework, integral psychology explores the depths of the psyche and the various dimensions of human experience, while integral spirituality delves into the deeper dimensions of existence beyond the realm of the psyche. By integrating psychological and spiritual perspectives, individuals can embark on a transformative journey of self-discovery, healing, and awakening, leading to greater wholeness, authenticity, and fulfillment in all aspects of their lives.

Integral Theory Approach to Psychology

Integral Theory offers a unique and comprehensive approach to psychology, presenting a holistic framework that encompasses various dimensions of human experience and development. Developed by philosopher Ken Wilber, Integral Theory draws upon insights from psychology, philosophy, spirituality, and other disciplines to provide a sophisticated understanding of the human psyche. By integrating multiple perspectives and dimensions, the Integral Theory approach to psychology offers valuable insights into the complexity of human consciousness and behavior.

At the heart of Integral Theory's approach to psychology is the AQAL framework, which stands for All Quadrants, All Levels. This framework provides a comprehensive map of reality, considering both subjective and objective, individual and collective aspects of human experience. By incorporating multiple dimensions such as quadrants, levels, lines, and states, the Integral Theory approach to psychology offers a more nuanced understanding of human consciousness and development.

One of the key insights of Integral Theory's approach to psychology is the recognition of multiple levels of development. These levels represent stages of cognitive, emotional, and moral growth that individuals progress through over time. Integral psychologists emphasize the importance of understanding and honoring each individual's unique developmental trajectory, recognizing that personal growth is an ongoing process that unfolds across the lifespan.

Integral Theory's approach to psychology also emphasizes the importance of considering multiple lines of development. These lines represent different aspects or intelligences within individuals, such as cognitive, emotional, moral, and spiritual intelligence. By recognizing the existence of multiple lines of development, Integral psychologists highlight the richness and complexity of human potential, encouraging individuals to cultivate a holistic and balanced approach to personal growth and development.

Moreover, Integral Theory's approach to psychology places a strong emphasis on shadow work – the process of exploring and integrating unconscious aspects of the psyche. By shining a light on the shadow – those parts of ourselves that we repress or deny – individuals can uncover hidden patterns and wounds that may be blocking their growth and well-being. Through practices such as therapy, meditation, and self-reflection, individuals can engage in the transformative process of shadow integration, leading to greater wholeness and authenticity.

Integral Theory's approach to psychology also emphasizes the importance of integrating psychological insights with spiritual teachings and practices. Integral psychologists draw upon wisdom from various spiritual traditions to deepen their understanding of human consciousness and development. By incorporating spiritual perspectives into their work, Integral psychologists offer a more holistic approach to psychological healing and transformation.

In conclusion, Integral Theory offers a comprehensive and integrated approach to psychology, drawing upon insights from psychology, philosophy, spirituality, and other disciplines. By incorporating multiple perspectives and dimensions, the Integral Theory approach to psychology provides valuable insights into the complexity of human consciousness and behavior. Through its emphasis on levels of development, lines of development, shadow work, and integration of psychological and spiritual perspectives, Integral Theory offers a transformative framework for understanding and navigating the depths of the human psyche.

Role of Spirituality in Integral Theory

Spirituality holds a central and integral role within Integral Theory, a comprehensive framework developed by philosopher Ken Wilber. Integral Theory offers a sophisticated approach to understanding human consciousness and development, incorporating insights from various disciplines such as psychology, philosophy, and spirituality. In Integral Theory, spirituality is not seen as separate from other dimensions of human experience but rather as an essential aspect that contributes to a holistic understanding of reality.

One of the key aspects of spirituality within Integral Theory is its recognition of the transcendent or spiritual dimensions of existence. Integral Theory acknowledges that human beings are not only physical, emotional, and mental beings but also spiritual beings with a deep longing for connection with something greater than themselves. This recognition of the spiritual dimension of human experience allows Integral Theory to offer a more holistic perspective on reality, one that embraces both the immanent and transcendent aspects of existence.

Moreover, Integral Theory emphasizes the importance of integrating spiritual insights and practices into everyday life. Rather than relegating spirituality to isolated practices or beliefs, Integral Theory encourages individuals to embody spiritual principles in all aspects of their lives. This integration of spirituality into daily life is often referred to as integral life practice, which encompasses physical, cognitive, spiritual, and relational practices aimed at fostering holistic well-being.

Integral Theory also emphasizes the importance of honoring and embracing the diversity of spiritual paths and traditions. Integral practitioners draw inspiration from a wide range of spiritual teachings and practices, recognizing that each tradition offers unique insights into the nature of reality and the human experience. By cultivating an attitude of openness, curiosity, and reverence towards different spiritual perspectives, individuals can deepen their understanding of themselves and the world around them.

Furthermore, Integral Theory recognizes the transformative potential of spiritual experiences and states of consciousness. Integral psychologists and spiritual teachers often draw upon practices such as meditation, contemplation, and mindfulness to facilitate experiences of expanded awareness and connection with the divine. These experiences can lead to profound insights, healing, and personal transformation, helping individuals to awaken to their true nature and purpose.

Integral Theory also emphasizes the importance of integrating psychological and spiritual perspectives. Integral psychologists draw upon insights from both psychology and spirituality to deepen their understanding of human consciousness and development. By integrating psychological and spiritual perspectives, Integral psychologists offer a more holistic approach to psychological healing and transformation, one that addresses the deeper dimensions of the human psyche and soul.

In conclusion, spirituality plays a central and integral role within Integral Theory, contributing to a holistic understanding of human consciousness and development. Integral Theory recognizes the transcendent dimensions of human experience and emphasizes the importance of integrating spiritual insights and practices into everyday life. By honoring the diversity of spiritual paths and traditions, cultivating spiritual experiences and states of consciousness, and integrating psychological and spiritual perspectives, Integral Theory offers a transformative framework for understanding and navigating the depths of the human psyche and soul.

Linking Psychology and Spirituality in Integral Theory

In Integral Theory, the linkage between psychology and spirituality is not merely a theoretical concept but a fundamental aspect that underpins the holistic understanding of human consciousness and development. Developed by philosopher Ken Wilber, Integral Theory provides a comprehensive framework that integrates insights from psychology, philosophy, spirituality, and other disciplines. By bridging the gap between psychology and spirituality, Integral Theory offers a nuanced perspective on the complexity of human experience.

At the heart of the linkage between psychology and spirituality in Integral Theory is the recognition that human beings are multifaceted beings with physical, emotional, mental, and spiritual dimensions. Integral Theory acknowledges that both psychology and spirituality play crucial roles in understanding and navigating the depths of the human psyche and soul.

Psychology, as a scientific discipline, focuses on understanding human behavior, cognition, and emotions. It explores the workings of the mind and the intricacies of human development. Integral psychology, within the framework of Integral Theory, considers multiple dimensions such as individual and collective, subjective and objective, in its exploration of human consciousness and behavior. By incorporating insights from psychology, Integral Theory offers valuable tools and methodologies for understanding and addressing psychological issues and challenges.

Spirituality, on the other hand, delves into the deeper dimensions of human experience beyond the realm of the psyche. It explores questions of meaning, purpose, and connection with something greater than oneself. Integral spirituality, within the framework of Integral Theory, draws upon wisdom from various spiritual traditions to deepen its understanding of human consciousness and development. By incorporating spiritual perspectives, Integral Theory offers insights into the transcendent dimensions of human existence and the transformative potential of spiritual experiences.

The linkage between psychology and spirituality in Integral Theory is evident in its approach to personal growth and transformation. Integral psychologists recognize the importance of integrating psychological insights with spiritual practices to facilitate healing and self-discovery. By combining therapeutic techniques with spiritual teachings,

Integral psychologists offer a holistic approach to psychological healing and transformation.

Moreover, Integral Theory emphasizes the importance of shadow work – the process of exploring and integrating unconscious aspects of the psyche – in the journey of personal growth and development. By shining a light on the shadow – those parts of ourselves that we repress or deny – individuals can uncover hidden patterns and wounds that may be blocking their growth and well-being. Through practices such as therapy, meditation, and self-reflection, individuals can engage in the transformative process of shadow integration, leading to greater wholeness and authenticity.

In conclusion, the linkage between psychology and spirituality in Integral Theory is essential for understanding the complexity of human consciousness and development. By bridging the gap between these two disciplines, Integral Theory offers a comprehensive framework that integrates insights from psychology and spirituality to foster personal growth, healing, and transformation. As individuals and societies continue to navigate the complexities of the modern world, the linkage between psychology and spirituality in Integral Theory remains a valuable resource for fostering understanding, empathy, and positive change.

Integral Theory in Leadership

Integral Theory offers a transformative approach to leadership, providing a comprehensive framework that integrates insights from various disciplines such as psychology, philosophy, and spirituality. Developed by philosopher Ken Wilber, Integral Theory recognizes that effective leadership requires a deep understanding of the complexity of human consciousness and development. By incorporating multiple perspectives and dimensions, Integral Theory offers valuable insights into the nature of leadership and the challenges facing leaders in today's world.

At the heart of Integral Theory's approach to leadership is the recognition of multiple dimensions of human experience. Integral Theory acknowledges that individuals are multifaceted beings with physical, emotional, mental, and spiritual dimensions, all of which interact and influence one another. Effective leaders must be able to navigate these dimensions skillfully, recognizing the diverse needs and capacities of their team members.

Integral Theory also emphasizes the importance of considering multiple perspectives in leadership. Integral leaders recognize that reality is multidimensional, encompassing both subjective and objective, individual and collective aspects. By incorporating insights from all quadrants – individual-interior, individual-exterior, collective-interior, and collective-exterior – Integral leaders gain a more comprehensive understanding of the complexities of the organizations and communities they lead.

Moreover, Integral Theory emphasizes the importance of recognizing and honoring the diversity of human experience. Integral leaders draw upon insights from various developmental models, recognizing that individuals and groups progress through stages of growth and evolution over time. By understanding and honoring each individual's unique developmental trajectory, Integral leaders can create environments that support growth, creativity, and innovation.

Integral Theory also emphasizes the importance of cultivating a balanced approach to leadership. Integral leaders recognize that effective leadership requires attention to multiple dimensions such as task orientation, relationship building, and personal development. By integrating these dimensions into their leadership approach, Integral leaders foster greater engagement, collaboration, and well-being among their team members.

Furthermore, Integral Theory emphasizes the importance of integrating personal and collective perspectives in leadership. Integral leaders recognize that effective leadership requires not only a deep understanding of individual psychology but also an awareness of the larger cultural and social contexts in which they operate. By integrating personal and collective perspectives, Integral leaders can create more inclusive and socially responsible organizations and communities.

Integral Theory also emphasizes the importance of ethical leadership. Integral leaders recognize that leadership is not just about achieving goals or maximizing profits but also about acting with integrity and compassion. By integrating ethical principles into their leadership approach, Integral leaders foster trust, respect, and loyalty among their team members and stakeholders.

In conclusion, Integral Theory offers a transformative approach to leadership, providing a comprehensive framework that integrates insights from psychology, philosophy, and spirituality. By recognizing the multidimensional nature of human experience, considering multiple perspectives, honoring diversity, cultivating a balanced approach, integrating personal and collective perspectives, and embracing ethical principles, Integral leaders can navigate the complexities of leadership with wisdom, compassion, and effectiveness. As organizations and communities continue to navigate the challenges of the modern world, Integral Theory offers valuable insights and tools for fostering positive change and transformation.

Introduction to Integral Leadership

Integral Leadership represents a transformative approach to guiding individuals, teams, and organizations towards success and fulfillment. Rooted in Integral Theory, a comprehensive framework developed by philosopher Ken Wilber, Integral Leadership offers a holistic perspective that integrates various dimensions of human experience and development.

At its core, Integral Leadership recognizes that effective leadership requires a deep understanding of the complexity of human consciousness and behavior. It acknowledges that individuals are multifaceted beings with physical, emotional, mental, and spiritual dimensions, all of which interact and influence one another. Integral Leadership emphasizes the importance of considering these multiple dimensions in guiding and inspiring others towards common goals.

One of the key principles of Integral Leadership is the recognition of multiple perspectives. Integral leaders understand that reality is multidimensional, encompassing both subjective and objective, individual and collective aspects. By incorporating insights from all quadrants – individual-interior, individual-exterior, collective-interior, and collective-exterior – Integral leaders gain a more comprehensive understanding of the contexts in which they operate.

Integral Leadership also emphasizes the importance of recognizing and honoring the diversity of human experience. Integral leaders draw upon insights from various developmental models, recognizing that individuals and groups progress through stages of growth and evolution over time. By understanding and honoring each individual's unique developmental trajectory, Integral leaders can create environments that support growth, creativity, and innovation.

Moreover, Integral Leadership emphasizes the importance of cultivating a balanced approach to leadership. Integral leaders recognize that effective leadership requires attention to multiple dimensions such as task orientation, relationship building, and personal development. By integrating these dimensions into their leadership approach, Integral leaders foster greater engagement, collaboration, and well-being among their team members.

Integral Leadership also emphasizes the importance of ethical leadership. Integral leaders recognize that leadership is not just about achieving goals or maximizing profits but also about acting with integrity and compassion. By integrating ethical principles into their leadership approach, Integral leaders foster trust, respect, and loyalty among their team members and stakeholders.

Integral Leadership also recognizes the interconnectedness of personal and collective perspectives. Integral leaders understand that effective leadership requires not only a deep understanding of individual psychology but also an awareness of the larger cultural and social contexts in which they operate. By integrating personal and collective perspectives, Integral leaders can create more inclusive and socially responsible organizations and communities.

In conclusion, Integral Leadership represents a transformative approach to guiding individuals, teams, and organizations towards success and fulfillment. By integrating insights from psychology, philosophy, and spirituality, Integral Leadership offers a holistic perspective that considers the complexity of human experience and development. As organizations and communities continue to navigate the challenges of the modern world, Integral Leadership offers valuable insights and tools for fostering positive change and transformation.

Exploring Leadership Styles in Integral theory

Integral Theory offers a nuanced perspective on leadership styles, recognizing that effective leadership is not a one-size-fits-all approach but rather a dynamic interplay of various styles, each with its strengths and limitations. Rooted in Integral Theory's comprehensive framework, the exploration of leadership styles encompasses an understanding of the complexity of human consciousness and development.

One of the foundational principles of Integral Theory's approach to leadership styles is the recognition of multiple perspectives. Integral leaders understand that reality is multifaceted, encompassing both subjective and objective, individual and collective aspects. This recognition leads to the understanding that there is no singular "best" leadership style, but rather a range of styles that may be appropriate depending on the context and circumstances.

One prominent leadership style within Integral Theory is authoritative leadership. This style is characterized by a clear vision and direction set by the leader, who inspires and motivates others to achieve common goals. While authoritative leadership can be effective in providing direction and guidance, Integral Theory recognizes that it may also be limited in its ability to foster collaboration and innovation if not balanced with other leadership styles.

Another leadership style explored in Integral Theory is participative or democratic leadership. This style emphasizes collaboration and inclusivity, with decisions made through consensus or consultation with team members. Participative leadership fosters a sense of ownership and empowerment among team members, leading to greater engagement and creativity. However, Integral Theory acknowledges that participative leadership may also be challenging in situations where quick decisions are required.

Transactional leadership is another leadership style explored within Integral Theory. This style is characterized by a focus on exchange and negotiation, with leaders providing rewards or incentives to motivate performance. Transactional leadership can be effective in clarifying expectations and maintaining accountability, but Integral Theory recognizes that it may also be limited in its ability to inspire intrinsic motivation and long-term commitment.

Transformational leadership is a leadership style that is highly valued within Integral Theory. This style emphasizes vision, inspiration, and personal development, with leaders inspiring and empowering others to reach their full potential. Transformational leaders foster a sense of purpose and meaning among team members, leading to greater commitment and innovation. However, Integral Theory acknowledges that transformational leadership may also be challenging to sustain over the long term.

Integral Theory also explores the concept of servant leadership, which emphasizes empathy, humility, and service to others. Servant leaders prioritize the well-being and growth of their team members, working to create environments that support their development and success. Integral Theory recognizes the transformative potential of servant leadership, as it fosters trust, collaboration, and a sense of community among team members.

In conclusion, Integral Theory offers a comprehensive framework for exploring leadership styles, recognizing the complexity of human consciousness and development. By understanding and integrating various leadership styles – including authoritative, participative, transactional, transformational, and servant leadership – Integral leaders can adapt their approach to meet the diverse needs and circumstances of their teams and organizations. As organizations and communities continue to navigate the complexities of the modern world, Integral Theory offers valuable insights and tools for fostering effective leadership and positive change.

Case Studies of Integral Leadership

Integral Theory offers a wealth of insights into effective leadership practices through case studies that exemplify the application of its principles in various contexts. These case studies showcase how Integral Theory's holistic framework can inform leadership decisions and strategies, leading to positive outcomes for individuals, organizations, and communities.

One notable case study of Integral Leadership is the transformation of Interface Inc., a global carpet manufacturer, under the leadership of Ray Anderson. Anderson, inspired by Integral Theory's emphasis on sustainability and social responsibility, embarked on a journey to transform Interface into a model of sustainable business practices. By integrating principles of environmental stewardship, social equity, and economic viability, Anderson successfully reimagined Interface's business model, leading to increased profitability and environmental impact reduction. This case study illustrates how Integral Leadership can inspire transformative change and innovation in organizations.

Another compelling case study of Integral Leadership is the story of Nelson Mandela's leadership during South Africa's transition from apartheid to democracy. Mandela's approach to leadership exemplified many principles of Integral Theory, including inclusivity, reconciliation, and visionary leadership. By embracing a spirit of forgiveness and reconciliation, Mandela was able to unite a divided nation and guide South Africa towards a peaceful transition to democracy. Mandela's leadership demonstrates how Integral Leadership can foster healing, reconciliation, and social change on a national scale.

In the field of education, the case study of the High Tech High charter schools in California provides an example of Integral Leadership in action. Founded by Larry Rosenstock, High Tech High is dedicated to providing a rigorous and innovative education that prepares students for success in the 21st century. Rosenstock's leadership approach emphasizes collaboration, creativity, and student-centered learning, drawing upon insights from Integral Theory to inform curriculum design and instructional practices. The success of High Tech High schools demonstrates how Integral Leadership can foster innovation and excellence in education.

In the realm of healthcare, the case study of the Cleveland Clinic under the leadership of Dr. Toby Cosgrove illustrates how Integral Leadership can drive organizational excellence and patient-centered care. Cosgrove's leadership approach emphasizes a holistic view of healthcare that integrates medical expertise with compassion, empathy, and patient empowerment. By focusing on quality improvement, innovation, and employee engagement, Cosgrove transformed the Cleveland Clinic into a world-renowned healthcare institution known for its commitment to excellence and patient satisfaction. This case study demonstrates how Integral Leadership can enhance healthcare delivery and improve patient outcomes.

Finally, the case study of Bhutan's Gross National Happiness (GNH) Index provides an example of Integral Leadership at the national level. Inspired by Integral Theory's emphasis on well-being and holistic development, the government of Bhutan introduced the GNH Index as an alternative measure of progress and prosperity. By prioritizing happiness and well-being over economic growth, Bhutan has become a global leader in sustainable development and well-being. This case study highlights how Integral Leadership can inform policy decisions and promote human flourishing at the societal level.

In conclusion, case studies of Integral Leadership demonstrate its transformative potential in various contexts, from business and education to healthcare and governance. By integrating principles of inclusivity, sustainability, and well-being, Integral Leadership offers a holistic approach to leadership that inspires positive change and fosters innovation, collaboration, and social impact. As leaders continue to navigate the complexities of the modern world, Integral Theory offers valuable insights and tools for fostering effective leadership and creating a better future for all.

Integral Ecology

Integral Ecology is a concept that emerges from Integral Theory, a comprehensive framework developed by philosopher Ken Wilber. Integral Ecology represents a holistic approach to understanding and addressing environmental challenges, recognizing the interconnectedness of human society, culture, and the natural world. By integrating insights from ecology, psychology, spirituality, and other disciplines, Integral Ecology offers a transformative perspective on environmental stewardship and sustainability.

One of the key principles of Integral Ecology is the recognition of the interconnectedness of all living beings and ecosystems. Integral theorists understand that human well-being is intimately linked to the health of the planet, and that environmental degradation affects not only the natural world but also human societies and cultures. By acknowledging these interconnections, Integral Ecology seeks to foster a deeper sense of ecological awareness and responsibility among individuals and communities.

Integral Ecology also emphasizes the importance of considering multiple perspectives in addressing environmental challenges. Integral theorists draw upon insights from various disciplines – including ecology, sociology, economics, and spirituality – to gain a more comprehensive understanding of the complexities of environmental issues. By integrating these diverse perspectives, Integral Ecology offers innovative solutions that address the root causes of environmental degradation and promote sustainability.

Moreover, Integral Ecology recognizes the importance of addressing environmental challenges at multiple levels – individual, collective, and systemic. Integral theorists understand that meaningful change requires action at all levels of society, from individual lifestyle choices to institutional and policy changes. By engaging individuals, communities, and governments in collaborative efforts, Integral Ecology seeks to create a more sustainable and resilient world for future generations.

Integral Ecology also emphasizes the importance of inner transformation as a catalyst for environmental change. Integral theorists recognize that ecological awareness and responsibility are deeply interconnected with personal growth and spiritual development. By cultivating mindfulness, compassion, and reverence for the natural world, individuals can deepen their connection to the Earth and become more effective agents of positive change.

One practical application of Integral Ecology is the concept of sustainable development, which seeks to meet the needs of the present generation without compromising the ability of future generations to meet their own needs. Integral theorists advocate for a holistic approach to sustainable development that considers environmental, social, and economic factors in decision-making processes. By integrating ecological principles with social justice and economic equity, Integral Ecology offers a framework for creating thriving and resilient communities.

Another key aspect of Integral Ecology is the recognition of the importance of diversity in ecosystems and human societies. Integral theorists understand that biodiversity and cultural diversity are essential for the health and resilience of both natural and human systems. By valuing and preserving diverse ecosystems, cultures, and ways of life, Integral Ecology seeks to promote resilience and sustainability in the face of environmental and social change.

In conclusion, Integral Ecology offers a transformative perspective on environmental stewardship and sustainability, integrating insights from ecology, psychology, spirituality, and other disciplines. By recognizing the interconnectedness of all living beings and ecosystems, considering multiple perspectives, addressing environmental challenges at multiple levels, fostering inner transformation, and valuing diversity, Integral Ecology offers a holistic approach to creating a more sustainable and resilient world for all. As individuals and communities continue to navigate the complexities of the modern world, Integral Ecology offers valuable insights and tools for fostering environmental awareness, responsibility, and action.

Understanding Integral Ecology

Integral Ecology is a profound concept that emerges from Integral Theory, a comprehensive framework developed by philosopher Ken Wilber. It represents a holistic approach to understanding and addressing environmental challenges, recognizing the intricate interconnectedness between human societies, cultures, and the natural world. Integral Ecology is not merely about preserving ecosystems or conserving resources; it encompasses a deeper understanding of the complex relationships between human beings and their environment.

At its core, Integral Ecology recognizes that human well-being is intricately tied to the health of the planet. It acknowledges that environmental degradation not only harms the natural world but also impacts human societies and cultures in profound ways. Thus, Integral Ecology seeks to foster a deeper sense of ecological awareness and responsibility among individuals and communities.

One of the fundamental principles of Integral Ecology is the recognition of the interconnectedness of all living beings and ecosystems. This interconnectedness is often depicted using the metaphor of the "web of life," where every organism and ecosystem is interconnected and interdependent. Integral Ecology acknowledges that actions taken in one part of the world can have far-reaching consequences for ecosystems and communities thousands of miles away.

Integral Ecology also emphasizes the importance of considering multiple perspectives in addressing environmental challenges. It draws upon insights from various disciplines, including ecology, sociology, economics, psychology, and spirituality, to gain a more comprehensive understanding of the complexities of environmental issues. By integrating these diverse perspectives, Integral Ecology offers innovative solutions that address the root causes of environmental degradation and promote sustainability.

Moreover, Integral Ecology recognizes the importance of addressing environmental challenges at multiple levels – individual, collective, and systemic. While individual actions such as recycling or reducing energy consumption are important, Integral Ecology emphasizes the need for broader systemic changes at the societal and global levels. This includes policy changes, technological innovations, and shifts in cultural values and norms.

Integral Ecology also emphasizes the importance of inner transformation as a catalyst for environmental change. It recognizes that ecological awareness and responsibility are deeply interconnected with personal growth and spiritual development. By cultivating mindfulness, compassion, and reverence for the natural world, individuals can deepen their connection to the Earth and become more effective agents of positive change.

One practical application of Integral Ecology is the concept of sustainable development, which seeks to meet the needs of the present generation without compromising the ability of future generations to meet their own needs. Integral theorists advocate for a holistic approach to sustainable development that considers environmental, social, and economic factors in decision-making processes. By integrating ecological principles with social justice and economic equity, Integral Ecology offers a framework for creating thriving and resilient communities.

In conclusion, Integral Ecology offers a transformative perspective on environmental stewardship and sustainability. By recognizing the interconnectedness of all living beings and ecosystems, considering multiple perspectives, addressing environmental challenges at multiple levels, fostering inner transformation, and promoting sustainable development, Integral Ecology offers a holistic approach to creating a more harmonious relationship between human beings and the natural world. As individuals and communities continue to navigate the complexities of the modern world, Integral Ecology offers valuable insights and tools for fostering environmental awareness, responsibility, and action.

Importance of Integral Approach in Ecology

The Integral Approach in Ecology offers a holistic and comprehensive perspective that is increasingly recognized as essential for addressing the complex environmental challenges facing our planet. Rooted in Integral Theory, this approach emphasizes the interconnectedness of all aspects of the natural world and human societies, recognizing that effective solutions to environmental issues require an understanding of the interplay between ecological, social, cultural, economic, and spiritual factors.

One of the key reasons for the importance of the Integral Approach in Ecology is its ability to transcend disciplinary boundaries and integrate insights from various fields of study. Traditional approaches to ecology often focus solely on biological and ecological factors, overlooking the social, cultural, and psychological dimensions of environmental issues. In contrast, the Integral Approach recognizes the interconnectedness of these dimensions and seeks to integrate them into a unified framework for understanding and addressing environmental challenges.

Moreover, the Integral Approach in Ecology emphasizes the importance of considering multiple perspectives in environmental decision-making. By drawing upon insights from ecology, sociology, economics, psychology, and spirituality, this approach offers a more comprehensive understanding of the root causes of environmental degradation and the potential solutions. For example, while ecological science may provide valuable information about biodiversity loss, an Integral Approach would also consider the social and economic factors driving deforestation or habitat destruction.

Furthermore, the Integral Approach in Ecology emphasizes the importance of addressing environmental challenges at multiple levels – individual, collective, and systemic. While individual actions such as recycling or reducing energy consumption are important, they are not sufficient to address the scale of the environmental crisis we face. Instead, the Integral Approach advocates for broader systemic changes at the societal and global levels, including policy changes, technological innovations, and shifts in cultural values and norms.

Integral Ecology also highlights the importance of inner transformation as a catalyst for environmental change. It recognizes that ecological awareness and responsibility are deeply interconnected with personal growth and spiritual development. By cultivating mindfulness, compassion, and reverence for the natural world, individuals can deepen their connection to the Earth and become more effective agents of positive change.

Furthermore, the Integral Approach in Ecology emphasizes the importance of diversity in ecosystems and human societies. It acknowledges that biodiversity and cultural diversity are essential for the health and resilience of both natural and human systems. By valuing and preserving diverse ecosystems, cultures, and ways of life, the Integral Approach promotes resilience and sustainability in the face of environmental and social change.

In conclusion, the Integral Approach in Ecology is of paramount importance for addressing the complex environmental challenges facing our planet. By transcending disciplinary boundaries, integrating multiple perspectives, addressing environmental challenges at multiple levels, fostering inner transformation, and valuing diversity, the Integral Approach offers a holistic framework for understanding and addressing environmental issues. As we continue to navigate the complexities of the modern world, the Integral Approach in Ecology provides valuable insights and tools for fostering environmental awareness, responsibility, and action.

Relationship between Ecology and Integral Theory

The relationship between Ecology and Integral Theory is one that encapsulates the interconnectedness of the natural world and human consciousness. Integral Theory, developed by philosopher Ken Wilber, provides a comprehensive framework that seeks to understand the complexities of human experience and development. Ecology, on the other hand, is the scientific study of the relationships between organisms and their environment. While seemingly distinct fields, the relationship between Ecology and Integral Theory is profound, as both offer complementary perspectives that contribute to a deeper understanding of the interconnectedness of all life forms and systems on Earth.

Integral Theory offers a holistic perspective on the relationship between humans and their environment, emphasizing the interdependence of all living beings and ecosystems. Integral theorists recognize that human well-being is intimately linked to the health of the planet and that environmental degradation can have far-reaching consequences for societies and cultures. By acknowledging this interconnectedness, Integral Theory fosters a deeper sense of ecological awareness and responsibility among individuals and communities.

Moreover, Integral Theory provides a framework for integrating insights from various disciplines into a unified understanding of environmental issues. This interdisciplinary approach is crucial for addressing the multifaceted nature of environmental challenges, which often transcend the boundaries of traditional scientific disciplines. By drawing upon insights from ecology, sociology, economics, psychology, and spirituality, Integral Theory offers innovative solutions that consider the social, cultural, economic, and psychological dimensions of environmental issues.

Integral Theory also emphasizes the importance of considering multiple perspectives in understanding and addressing environmental challenges. Integral theorists recognize that reality is multifaceted, encompassing both subjective and objective, individual and collective aspects. By integrating insights from all quadrants – individual-interior, individual-exterior, collective-interior, and collective-exterior – Integral Theory offers a more comprehensive understanding of the complexities of environmental issues.

Furthermore, Integral Theory emphasizes the importance of addressing environmental challenges at multiple levels – individual, collective, and systemic. While individual actions such as recycling or reducing energy consumption are important, they are not sufficient to address the scale of the environmental crisis we face. Instead, Integral Theory advocates for broader systemic changes at the societal and global levels, including policy changes, technological innovations, and shifts in cultural values and norms.

Integral Theory also recognizes the importance of inner transformation as a catalyst for environmental change. It acknowledges that ecological awareness and responsibility are deeply interconnected with personal growth and spiritual development. By cultivating mindfulness, compassion, and reverence for the natural world, individuals can deepen their connection to the Earth and become more effective agents of positive change.

In conclusion, the relationship between Ecology and Integral Theory is one of profound interconnectedness and mutual enrichment. Integral Theory offers a holistic perspective that integrates insights from various disciplines into a unified understanding of environmental issues. By emphasizing the interconnectedness of all life forms and systems on Earth, considering multiple perspectives, addressing environmental challenges at multiple levels, fostering inner transformation, and valuing diversity, Integral Theory provides a powerful framework for understanding and addressing environmental challenges in the modern world.

Integral Theory in Education

Integral Theory has gained significant traction in the realm of education, offering a comprehensive framework that addresses the diverse needs and complexities of learning and development. Developed by philosopher Ken Wilber, Integral Theory provides a holistic perspective that integrates insights from various disciplines, including psychology, sociology, spirituality, and philosophy. Its application in education has led to innovative approaches that aim to nurture the intellectual, emotional, social, and spiritual dimensions of students.

One of the key aspects of Integral Theory in education is its recognition of the multiple dimensions of human development. Integral theorists understand that individuals are multifaceted beings with physical, emotional, mental, and spiritual dimensions, all of which interact and influence one another. This understanding informs teaching practices that seek to address the diverse needs and potentials of students across these dimensions.

Moreover, Integral Theory emphasizes the importance of considering multiple perspectives in education. Integral educators draw upon insights from developmental psychology, cultural studies, and systems theory to gain a more comprehensive understanding of the complexities of learning and development. By integrating these diverse perspectives, Integral educators are able to design curriculum and pedagogy that are relevant, engaging, and effective.

Integral Theory also emphasizes the importance of addressing the whole child in education. Integral educators understand that learning is not just about acquiring knowledge and skills but also about fostering emotional intelligence, social competence, and ethical responsibility. This holistic approach to education seeks to nurture students' intellectual, emotional, and social development, preparing them to navigate the complexities of the modern world with wisdom and compassion.

Furthermore, Integral Theory recognizes the importance of addressing the cultural and social dimensions of education. Integral educators understand that education is deeply influenced by cultural values, norms, and beliefs, and that these factors play a significant role in shaping students' identities and experiences. By integrating insights from cultural studies and sociology, Integral educators are able to create learning environments that are inclusive, diverse, and culturally responsive.

Integral Theory also emphasizes the importance of fostering critical thinking and creativity in education. Integral educators understand that students need to develop the ability to think independently, critically evaluate information, and creatively solve problems in order to thrive in the 21st century. By integrating insights from philosophy and cognitive psychology, Integral educators are able to design curriculum and pedagogy that stimulate students' intellectual curiosity and creativity.

In conclusion, Integral Theory offers a comprehensive framework that is highly relevant to education in the 21st century. By emphasizing the multiple dimensions of human development, considering multiple perspectives, addressing the whole child, acknowledging the cultural and social dimensions of education, and fostering critical thinking and creativity, Integral Theory provides valuable insights and tools for creating learning environments that are engaging, inclusive, and effective. As educators continue to navigate the complexities of the modern world, Integral Theory offers a powerful framework for promoting learning and development that is meaningful, relevant, and transformative.

Overview of Integral Education

Integral Education represents a transformative approach to teaching and learning that integrates insights from Integral Theory, a comprehensive framework developed by philosopher Ken Wilber. It offers a holistic perspective that addresses the diverse needs and potentials of students across multiple dimensions of human development, including intellectual, emotional, social, and spiritual. Integral Education has gained significant attention in recent years for its innovative approaches to curriculum design, pedagogy, and assessment.

One of the key principles of Integral Education is its recognition of the multiple dimensions of human development. Integral educators understand that individuals are multifaceted beings with physical, emotional, mental, and spiritual dimensions, all of which interact and influence one another. This understanding informs teaching practices that seek to address the diverse needs and potentials of students across these dimensions.

Integral Education also emphasizes the importance of considering multiple perspectives in teaching and learning. Integral educators draw upon insights from various disciplines, including psychology, sociology, spirituality, and philosophy, to gain a more comprehensive understanding of the complexities of human development and learning. By integrating these diverse perspectives, Integral educators are able to design curriculum and pedagogy that are relevant, engaging, and effective.

Moreover, Integral Education emphasizes the importance of addressing the whole student. Integral educators understand that education is not just about acquiring knowledge and skills but also about fostering emotional intelligence, social competence, and ethical responsibility. This holistic approach to education seeks to nurture students' intellectual, emotional, and social development, preparing them to navigate the complexities of the modern world with wisdom and compassion.

Integral Education also emphasizes the importance of fostering critical thinking and creativity. Integral educators understand that students need to develop the ability to think independently, critically evaluate information, and creatively solve problems in order to thrive in the 21st century. By integrating insights from philosophy and cognitive psychology, Integral educators are able to design curriculum and pedagogy that stimulate students' intellectual curiosity and creativity.

Integral Education also recognizes the importance of addressing the cultural and social dimensions of education. Integral educators understand that education is deeply influenced by cultural values, norms, and beliefs, and that these factors play a significant role in shaping students' identities and experiences. By integrating insights from cultural studies and sociology, Integral educators are able to create learning environments that are inclusive, diverse, and culturally responsive.

In conclusion, Integral Education offers a transformative approach to teaching and learning that is highly relevant to the challenges and opportunities of the 21st century. By emphasizing the multiple dimensions of human development, considering multiple perspectives, addressing the whole student, fostering critical thinking and creativity, and acknowledging the cultural and social dimensions of education, Integral Education provides valuable insights and tools for creating learning environments that are engaging, inclusive, and effective. As educators continue to navigate the complexities of the modern world, Integral Education offers a powerful framework for promoting learning and development that is meaningful, relevant, and transformative.

Integrating Theory in Curriculum Development

Integrating theory into curriculum development is a crucial aspect of creating educational programs that are comprehensive, effective, and responsive to the diverse needs of students. One theory that has gained significant attention in this regard is Integral Theory, developed by philosopher Ken Wilber. Integral Theory offers a holistic framework that integrates insights from various disciplines, including psychology, sociology, spirituality, and philosophy. By incorporating Integral Theory into curriculum development, educators can create learning experiences that address the multiple dimensions of human development and foster a deeper understanding of the interconnectedness of knowledge and experience.

One of the key benefits of integrating Integral Theory into curriculum development is its emphasis on addressing the whole student. Integral Theory recognizes that individuals are multifaceted beings with physical, emotional, mental, and spiritual dimensions, all of which interact and influence one another. By incorporating this understanding into curriculum design, educators can create learning experiences that nurture students' intellectual, emotional, and social development, preparing them to navigate the complexities of the modern world with wisdom and compassion.

Moreover, integrating Integral Theory into curriculum development allows educators to consider multiple perspectives in teaching and learning. Integral Theory draws upon insights from various disciplines to gain a more comprehensive understanding of human development and learning. By incorporating these diverse perspectives into curriculum design, educators can create learning experiences that are relevant, engaging, and effective for a wide range of students.

Integral Theory also emphasizes the importance of fostering critical thinking and creativity in education. By integrating insights from philosophy and cognitive psychology, educators can design curriculum and pedagogy that stimulate students' intellectual curiosity and creativity. This approach to curriculum development encourages students to think independently, critically evaluate information, and creatively solve problems, preparing them to thrive in the 21st century.

Furthermore, integrating Integral Theory into curriculum development allows educators to address the cultural and social dimensions of education. Integral Theory recognizes that education is deeply influenced by cultural values, norms, and beliefs, and that these factors play a significant role in shaping students' identities and experiences. By incorporating insights from cultural studies and sociology, educators can create learning environments that are inclusive, diverse, and culturally responsive.

In conclusion, integrating theory into curriculum development is essential for creating educational programs that are comprehensive, effective, and responsive to the diverse needs of students. Integral Theory offers a holistic framework that integrates insights from various disciplines to provide a deeper understanding of human development and learning. By incorporating Integral Theory into curriculum development, educators can create learning experiences that address the whole student, consider multiple perspectives, foster critical thinking and creativity, and address the cultural and social dimensions of education. As educators continue to navigate the complexities of the modern world, integrating theory into curriculum development offers a powerful tool for promoting learning and development that is meaningful, relevant, and transformative.

Pedagogical Implications of Integral Theory

The Pedagogical Implications of Integral Theory offer a profound framework for educators to enhance teaching practices and foster holistic student development. Integral Theory, developed by philosopher Ken Wilber, provides a comprehensive framework that integrates insights from various disciplines, including psychology, sociology, spirituality, and philosophy. By incorporating Integral Theory into pedagogy, educators can create learning experiences that address the diverse needs and potentials of students across multiple dimensions of human development.

One of the key pedagogical implications of Integral Theory is its emphasis on addressing the whole student. Integral theorists recognize that individuals are multifaceted beings with physical, emotional, mental, and spiritual dimensions, all of which interact and influence one another. This understanding informs teaching practices that seek to nurture students' intellectual, emotional, social, and spiritual development, preparing them to navigate the complexities of the modern world with wisdom and compassion.

Moreover, Integral Theory emphasizes the importance of considering multiple perspectives in teaching and learning. Integral educators draw upon insights from various disciplines to gain a more comprehensive understanding of human development and learning. By integrating these diverse perspectives into pedagogy, educators can design learning experiences that are relevant, engaging, and effective for a wide range of students.

Integral Theory also highlights the importance of fostering critical thinking and creativity in education. By integrating insights from philosophy and cognitive psychology, educators can design curriculum and pedagogy that stimulate students' intellectual curiosity and creativity. This approach encourages students to think independently, critically evaluate information, and creatively solve problems, preparing them to thrive in the 21st century.

Furthermore, Integral Theory emphasizes the importance of addressing the cultural and social dimensions of education. Integral educators understand that education is deeply influenced by cultural values, norms, and beliefs, and that these factors play a significant role in shaping students' identities and experiences. By incorporating insights from cultural studies and sociology, educators can create learning environments that are inclusive, diverse, and culturally responsive.

Integral Theory also recognizes the importance of fostering self-awareness and mindfulness in education. Integral educators understand that self-awareness and mindfulness are essential for students to develop a deeper understanding of themselves and their place in the world. By incorporating practices such as meditation, reflection, and contemplation into pedagogy, educators can help students cultivate inner peace, clarity, and compassion, enhancing their overall well-being and resilience.

In conclusion, the pedagogical implications of Integral Theory offer a transformative approach to teaching and learning that is highly relevant to the challenges and opportunities of the 21st century. By emphasizing the whole student, considering multiple perspectives, fostering critical thinking and creativity, addressing the cultural and social dimensions of education, and fostering self-awareness and mindfulness, Integral Theory provides valuable insights and tools for creating learning experiences that are engaging, inclusive, and effective. As educators continue to navigate the complexities of the modern world, the pedagogical implications of Integral Theory offer a powerful framework for promoting holistic student development that is meaningful, relevant, and transformative.

Business and Organization Development through Integral Theory

Business and organization development through Integral Theory presents a transformative approach to enhancing organizational effectiveness and fostering sustainable growth. Integral Theory, developed by philosopher Ken Wilber, provides a comprehensive framework that integrates insights from various disciplines, including psychology, sociology, spirituality, and philosophy. By incorporating Integral Theory into business and organization development, leaders and managers can gain a deeper understanding of the complexities of organizational dynamics and implement strategies that address the diverse needs and potentials of employees and stakeholders.

One of the key principles of business and organization development through Integral Theory is its recognition of the multiple dimensions of organizational life. Integral theorists understand that organizations are complex systems with physical, social, cultural, and psychological dimensions, all of which interact and influence one another. This understanding informs organizational development practices that seek to address the diverse needs and potentials of employees and stakeholders across these dimensions.

Moreover, Integral Theory emphasizes the importance of considering multiple perspectives in organizational development. Integral practitioners draw upon insights from various disciplines to gain a more comprehensive understanding of organizational dynamics and effectiveness. By integrating these diverse perspectives into organizational development practices, leaders and managers can design strategies that are relevant, engaging, and effective for a wide range of employees and stakeholders.

Integral Theory also highlights the importance of fostering collaboration and synergy in organizations. By recognizing the interconnectedness of all aspects of organizational life, Integral practitioners seek to create environments that foster cooperation, creativity, and innovation. This approach encourages employees and stakeholders to work together towards common goals, maximizing the organization's potential for success.

Furthermore, Integral Theory emphasizes the importance of addressing the cultural and social dimensions of organizations. Integral practitioners understand that organizational culture, values, and norms play a significant role in shaping employees' attitudes, behaviors, and performance. By incorporating insights from cultural studies and sociology, leaders and managers can create organizational cultures that are inclusive, diverse, and supportive of employee well-being and growth.

Integral Theory also recognizes the importance of fostering individual and collective development in organizations. Integral practitioners understand that employees and stakeholders need opportunities for personal and professional growth in order to thrive in the modern workplace. By incorporating practices such as coaching, mentoring, and leadership development into organizational development strategies, leaders and managers can support the ongoing growth and development of employees and stakeholders, enhancing organizational effectiveness and resilience.

In conclusion, business and organization development through Integral Theory offers a transformative approach to enhancing organizational effectiveness and fostering sustainable growth. By emphasizing the multiple dimensions of organizational life, considering multiple perspectives, fostering collaboration and synergy, addressing the cultural and social dimensions of organizations, and fostering individual and collective development, Integral Theory provides valuable insights and tools for creating organizations that are dynamic, adaptive, and resilient in the face of change. As leaders and managers continue to navigate the complexities of the modern business landscape, the principles of Integral Theory offer a powerful framework for promoting organizational success and well-being.

Role of Integral Theory in Business Management

Integral Theory has emerged as a significant framework in the realm of business management, offering a holistic approach that addresses the complexities of modern organizational dynamics. Developed by philosopher Ken Wilber, Integral Theory integrates insights from various disciplines such as psychology, sociology, spirituality, and philosophy. Its application in business management provides leaders and managers with a comprehensive framework to navigate the multifaceted challenges of the corporate world and foster sustainable success.

One of the primary roles of Integral Theory in business management is its emphasis on addressing the multiple dimensions of organizational life. Integral theorists recognize that organizations are complex systems with physical, social, cultural, and psychological dimensions, all of which interact and influence one another. By incorporating this understanding into business management practices, leaders and managers can develop strategies that address the diverse needs and potentials of employees, customers, and stakeholders across these dimensions.

Moreover, Integral Theory emphasizes the importance of considering multiple perspectives in business management. Integral practitioners draw upon insights from various disciplines to gain a more comprehensive understanding of organizational dynamics and effectiveness. By integrating these diverse perspectives into management practices, leaders and managers can make informed decisions that are relevant, inclusive, and effective for all stakeholders.

Integral Theory also highlights the importance of fostering collaboration and synergy in organizations. By recognizing the interconnectedness of all aspects of organizational life, Integral practitioners seek to create environments that foster cooperation, creativity, and innovation. This approach encourages employees to work together towards common goals, maximizing the organization's potential for success and adaptability in an ever-changing business landscape.

Furthermore, Integral Theory emphasizes the importance of addressing the cultural and social dimensions of organizations. Integral practitioners understand that organizational culture, values, and norms play a significant role in shaping employee attitudes, behaviors, and performance. By incorporating insights from cultural studies and sociology, leaders and managers can create organizational cultures that are inclusive, diverse, and supportive of employee well-being and growth.

Integral Theory also recognizes the importance of fostering individual and collective development in organizations. Leaders and managers understand that employees and stakeholders need opportunities for personal and professional growth to thrive in the modern workplace. By incorporating practices such as coaching, mentoring, and leadership development into business management strategies, leaders can support ongoing growth and development, enhancing organizational effectiveness and resilience.

In conclusion, the role of Integral Theory in business management is multifaceted and essential for navigating the complexities of modern organizational dynamics. By emphasizing the multiple dimensions of organizational life, considering multiple perspectives, fostering collaboration and synergy, addressing the cultural and social dimensions of organizations, and fostering individual and collective development, Integral Theory provides valuable insights and tools for creating organizations that are dynamic, adaptive, and resilient in the face of change. As leaders and managers continue to navigate the challenges of the modern business landscape, the principles of Integral Theory offer a powerful framework for promoting organizational success and well-being.

Integral Approach to Organizational Development

The Integral Approach to Organizational Development represents a holistic and transformative framework for fostering growth, adaptability, and sustainability within organizations. Rooted in Integral Theory developed by philosopher Ken Wilber, this approach integrates insights from various disciplines including psychology, sociology, spirituality, and philosophy. By incorporating the Integral Approach into organizational development, businesses can address the multifaceted challenges of the modern corporate landscape and create environments conducive to success and innovation.

One of the fundamental principles of the Integral Approach to Organizational Development is its recognition of the interconnectedness and interdependence of all aspects of organizational life. Integral theorists understand that organizations are complex systems with physical, social, cultural, and psychological dimensions, all of which interact and influence one another. By acknowledging and addressing these dimensions, organizations can develop strategies that are comprehensive and effective in driving growth and progress.

Moreover, the Integral Approach emphasizes the importance of considering multiple perspectives in organizational development. Integral practitioners draw upon insights from various disciplines to gain a deeper understanding of organizational dynamics and effectiveness. By integrating these diverse perspectives, organizations can develop strategies that are inclusive, adaptive, and responsive to the needs of employees, customers, and stakeholders.

Integral Theory also highlights the importance of fostering collaboration and synergy within organizations. By recognizing the interconnectedness of all aspects of organizational life, Integral practitioners seek to create environments that encourage cooperation, creativity, and innovation. This approach encourages employees to work together towards common goals, maximizing the organization's potential for success and adaptability in an ever-changing business environment.

Furthermore, the Integral Approach emphasizes the importance of addressing the cultural and social dimensions of organizations. Integral practitioners understand that organizational culture, values, and norms play a significant role in shaping employee attitudes, behaviors, and performance. By incorporating insights from cultural studies and sociology, organizations can create cultures that are inclusive, diverse, and supportive of employee well-being and growth.

Integral Theory also recognizes the importance of fostering individual and collective development within organizations. Leaders and managers understand that employees and stakeholders need opportunities for personal and professional growth to thrive in the modern workplace. By incorporating practices such as coaching, mentoring, and leadership development into organizational development strategies, organizations can support ongoing growth and development, enhancing organizational effectiveness and resilience.

In conclusion, the Integral Approach to Organizational Development offers a comprehensive and transformative framework for fostering growth, adaptability, and sustainability within organizations. By emphasizing the interconnectedness of all aspects of organizational life, considering multiple perspectives, fostering collaboration and synergy, addressing the cultural and social dimensions of organizations, and fostering individual and collective development, the Integral Approach provides valuable insights and tools for creating organizations that are dynamic, adaptive, and resilient in the face of change. As organizations continue to navigate the challenges of the modern business landscape, the principles of the Integral Approach offer a powerful framework for promoting organizational success and well-being.

Business Case Studies using Integral Theory

Business case studies utilizing Integral Theory showcase the practical application and effectiveness of this comprehensive framework in addressing real-world organizational challenges. Integral Theory, developed by philosopher Ken Wilber, integrates insights from various disciplines such as psychology, sociology, spirituality, and philosophy. By incorporating Integral Theory into business management practices, companies can gain deeper insights into their operations and develop strategies that are holistic, inclusive, and sustainable.

One notable business case study that exemplifies the use of Integral Theory is the transformation of a multinational corporation's organizational culture. Facing challenges related to employee disengagement, low morale, and high turnover rates, the company sought to revitalize its corporate culture to improve productivity and retention. By applying Integral Theory, the company's leadership team recognized the need to address not only the external factors affecting employee satisfaction but also the internal dimensions such as individual values, beliefs, and motivations.

Through a series of initiatives informed by Integral Theory, including leadership development programs, team-building exercises, and cultural workshops, the company successfully transformed its organizational culture. By fostering collaboration, empathy, and shared purpose among employees, the company experienced a significant increase in employee engagement, job satisfaction, and retention rates. The integration of Integral Theory allowed the company to approach organizational change from a holistic perspective, addressing both the external and internal factors influencing employee well-being and performance.

Another compelling business case study demonstrating the efficacy of Integral Theory is the turnaround of a struggling startup company. Facing financial difficulties, market competition, and internal conflicts, the company was on the verge of bankruptcy. By adopting Integral Theory as a guiding framework for strategic planning and decision-making, the company's leadership team was able to identify and address the root causes of its challenges.

Utilizing Integral Theory, the company developed a comprehensive turnaround plan that addressed not only the external market conditions but also the internal organizational dynamics. By fostering open communication, trust, and collaboration among employees, the company was able to overcome internal conflicts and improve teamwork. Additionally, by integrating sustainability practices into its operations, the company enhanced its brand reputation and market competitiveness.

As a result of its strategic initiatives informed by Integral Theory, the company experienced a remarkable turnaround, achieving profitability and sustainable growth. By embracing Integral Theory, the company was able to navigate through its challenges with a holistic understanding of its business ecosystem, addressing the interconnectedness of external market forces and internal organizational dynamics.

Furthermore, Integral Theory has been applied in the context of corporate social responsibility (CSR) initiatives, as demonstrated by a case study of a multinational corporation's CSR program. By adopting an Integral approach to CSR, the company was able to go beyond traditional philanthropy and incorporate social, environmental, and ethical considerations into its business strategy. Through partnerships with local communities, environmental organizations, and governmental agencies, the company successfully implemented CSR initiatives that created value for both society and the business.

In conclusion, business case studies utilizing Integral Theory illustrate the transformative potential of this comprehensive framework in addressing real-world organizational challenges. By embracing Integral Theory, companies can gain deeper insights into their operations, develop strategies that are holistic and sustainable, and create value for both stakeholders and society. As businesses continue to navigate the complexities of the modern business landscape, Integral Theory offers a powerful framework for promoting organizational success and societal well-being.

Integral Theory and Social Movements

Integral Theory, a comprehensive framework developed by philosopher Ken Wilber, offers valuable insights into the dynamics of social movements and their impact on society. By integrating perspectives from various disciplines such as psychology, sociology, spirituality, and philosophy, Integral Theory provides a holistic understanding of the complex interplay between individual and collective factors driving social change.

One of the key contributions of Integral Theory to the study of social movements is its emphasis on addressing the multiple dimensions of human experience. Integral theorists recognize that social movements arise from a combination of individual motivations, cultural values, and systemic factors. By considering these dimensions in conjunction, Integral Theory offers a nuanced understanding of the underlying drivers of social change.

Moreover, Integral Theory emphasizes the importance of considering multiple perspectives in analyzing social movements. Integral theorists draw upon insights from diverse disciplines to gain a comprehensive understanding of the dynamics of social change. By integrating these perspectives, researchers can develop more holistic and inclusive theories of social movements that account for the complex interactions between individuals, communities, and institutions.

Integral Theory also highlights the role of developmental stages in shaping social movements. Integral theorists understand that individuals and societies evolve through various stages of psychological and moral development. By recognizing the influence of developmental factors on social change, Integral Theory provides insights into the emergence and evolution of different types of social movements over time.

Furthermore, Integral Theory emphasizes the interconnectedness of individual and collective dimensions in social movements. Integral theorists recognize that social movements are driven by both individual agency and collective action. By integrating insights from psychology and sociology, Integral Theory offers a holistic understanding of the complex interactions between individual motivations, group dynamics, and societal structures in driving social change.

Integral Theory also highlights the importance of addressing the cultural and systemic dimensions of social movements. Integral theorists understand that social movements are embedded within broader cultural and institutional contexts. By incorporating insights from cultural studies and political science, Integral Theory offers a comprehensive understanding of the social, economic, and political factors shaping the dynamics of social movements.

Moreover, Integral Theory recognizes the importance of fostering collaboration and dialogue among diverse stakeholders in social movements. Integral theorists understand that effective social change requires collective action and cooperation across different sectors of society. By emphasizing the importance of inclusivity and diversity, Integral Theory offers insights into how social movements can build alliances and coalitions to achieve their goals.

In conclusion, Integral Theory offers valuable insights into the dynamics of social movements and their impact on society. By integrating perspectives from various disciplines and emphasizing the interconnectedness of individual and collective dimensions, Integral Theory provides a comprehensive framework for understanding the complexities of social change. As researchers and activists continue to grapple with the challenges of promoting social justice and equality, Integral Theory offers a powerful tool for analyzing and addressing the underlying drivers of social movements.

Relationship between Social Movements and Integral Theory

The relationship between social movements and Integral Theory is a dynamic and multi-faceted one that offers valuable insights into the nature, dynamics, and impact of collective action for social change. Integral Theory, developed by philosopher Ken Wilber, provides a comprehensive framework that integrates perspectives from various disciplines, including psychology, sociology, spirituality, and philosophy. By applying Integral Theory to the study of social movements, researchers and activists can gain a deeper understanding of the complexities of collective action and its implications for societal transformation.

Integral Theory offers a holistic perspective on social movements, emphasizing the interconnectedness of individual and collective dimensions. Integral theorists recognize that social movements are driven by both individual motivations and collective aspirations. By integrating insights from psychology and sociology, Integral Theory provides a nuanced understanding of the factors influencing participation in social movements, including identity, ideology, and social networks.

Moreover, Integral Theory highlights the role of developmental stages in shaping social movements. Integral theorists understand that individuals and societies evolve through various stages of psychological and moral development. By recognizing the influence of developmental factors on social change, Integral Theory provides insights into the emergence and evolution of different types of social movements over time.

Integral Theory also emphasizes the importance of considering multiple perspectives in analyzing social movements. Integral theorists draw upon insights from diverse disciplines to gain a comprehensive understanding of the dynamics of social change. By integrating these perspectives, researchers can develop more holistic and inclusive theories of social movements that account for the complex interactions between individuals, communities, and institutions.

Furthermore, Integral Theory highlights the interconnectedness of social movements with broader cultural, economic, and political contexts. Integral theorists understand that social movements are embedded within larger systems of power and privilege. By incorporating insights from cultural studies and political science, Integral Theory offers a comprehensive understanding of the social, economic, and political factors shaping the dynamics of social movements.

Integral Theory also emphasizes the importance of fostering collaboration and dialogue among diverse stakeholders in social movements. Integral theorists understand that effective social change requires collective action and cooperation across different sectors of society. By emphasizing the importance of inclusivity and diversity, Integral Theory offers insights into how social movements can build alliances and coalitions to achieve their goals.

In conclusion, the relationship between social movements and Integral Theory is characterized by mutual enrichment and synergy. By applying Integral Theory to the study of social movements, researchers and activists can gain a deeper understanding of the complexities of collective action and its implications for societal transformation. As social movements continue to shape the course of history, Integral Theory offers a powerful framework for analyzing and addressing the underlying drivers of social change.

Examples of Integral Social Movements

Integral Theory, a comprehensive framework developed by philosopher Ken Wilber, has influenced various social movements worldwide, offering valuable insights into their dynamics and impacts. These Integral social movements incorporate the principles and perspectives of Integral Theory to address complex societal issues and promote holistic approaches to social change. Here are several examples of Integral social movements that illustrate the diverse applications and effectiveness of Integral Theory in addressing contemporary challenges:

Integral Sustainability Movement:
The Integral Sustainability Movement aims to address environmental, social, and economic issues through an integrated approach informed by Integral Theory. This movement recognizes the interconnectedness of environmental degradation, social injustice, and economic inequality and seeks to promote sustainable practices that address these issues simultaneously. Integral sustainability initiatives incorporate ecological stewardship, social equity, and economic prosperity, fostering holistic solutions that promote long-term well-being for both humanity and the planet.

Integral Education Movement:
The Integral Education Movement seeks to transform education systems by integrating Integral Theory principles into educational practices. This movement emphasizes the importance of addressing the cognitive, emotional, social, and spiritual dimensions of learning to nurture the holistic development of students. Integral education initiatives incorporate interdisciplinary curricula, experiential learning, and personal growth practices, empowering students to become engaged, compassionate, and socially responsible individuals.

Integral Health and Wellness Movement:
The Integral Health and Wellness Movement advocates for a holistic approach to health and well-being that addresses the physical, mental, emotional, and spiritual dimensions of human experience. This movement integrates insights from conventional medicine, alternative therapies, and mind-body practices to promote comprehensive wellness. Integral health initiatives focus on preventive care, lifestyle interventions, and self-care practices, empowering individuals to cultivate resilience, vitality, and wholeness.

Integral Social Justice Movement:

The Integral Social Justice Movement aims to address systemic oppression, discrimination, and inequality through an integrated approach informed by Integral Theory. This movement recognizes the intersectionality of social identities and experiences and seeks to promote justice, equity, and inclusivity for all marginalized communities. Integral social justice initiatives incorporate advocacy, allyship, and community organizing, fostering collective action to dismantle oppressive systems and create a more just and equitable society.

Integral Consciousness Evolution Movement:
The Integral Consciousness Evolution Movement focuses on personal and collective transformation through the development of higher states of consciousness informed by Integral Theory. This movement recognizes the potential for individuals and societies to evolve towards greater levels of awareness, compassion, and wisdom. Integral consciousness evolution initiatives include spiritual practices, meditation, and transformative learning experiences, facilitating the growth and evolution of human consciousness.

Overall, these examples demonstrate the diverse applications and impacts of Integral Theory in addressing contemporary societal challenges through social movements. By integrating Integral perspectives into their strategies and practices, these movements promote holistic approaches to social change that foster individual and collective well-being, sustainability, justice, and consciousness evolution. As Integral social movements continue to evolve and expand, they contribute to the ongoing transformation of society towards a more integrated, inclusive, and flourishing future.

The Future of Social Movements Under Integral Theory

The future of social movements under Integral Theory promises to be dynamic, transformative, and increasingly impactful as societies continue to grapple with complex challenges and opportunities. Integral Theory, developed by philosopher Ken Wilber, provides a comprehensive framework that integrates insights from various disciplines, including psychology, sociology, spirituality, and philosophy. By applying Integral Theory to the study and practice of social movements, activists, scholars, and practitioners can gain deeper insights into the nature, dynamics, and potential of collective action for social change.

One of the key implications of Integral Theory for the future of social movements is its emphasis on addressing the multiple dimensions of human experience. Integral theorists recognize that social movements arise from a combination of individual motivations, cultural values, and systemic factors. By considering these dimensions in conjunction, Integral Theory offers a holistic understanding of the underlying drivers of social change and the interconnectedness of individual and collective dimensions.

Moreover, Integral Theory highlights the importance of considering multiple perspectives in analyzing and addressing social issues. Integral theorists draw upon insights from diverse disciplines to gain a comprehensive understanding of the dynamics of social change. By integrating these perspectives, activists and organizers can develop more holistic and inclusive strategies that account for the complex interactions between individuals, communities, and institutions.

Integral Theory also emphasizes the role of developmental stages in shaping social movements. Integral theorists understand that individuals and societies evolve through various stages of psychological and moral development. By recognizing the influence of developmental factors on social change, Integral Theory provides insights into the emergence and evolution of different types of social movements over time and their potential for fostering personal and collective growth.

Furthermore, Integral Theory highlights the interconnectedness of social movements with broader cultural, economic, and political contexts. Integral theorists understand that social movements are embedded within larger systems of power and privilege. By incorporating insights from cultural studies and political science, Integral Theory offers a comprehensive understanding of the social, economic, and political factors shaping the dynamics of social movements and their potential to effect systemic change.

Integral Theory also emphasizes the importance of fostering collaboration and dialogue among diverse stakeholders in social movements. Effective social change requires collective action and cooperation across different sectors of society. By emphasizing the importance of inclusivity and diversity, Integral Theory offers insights into how social movements can build alliances and coalitions to achieve their goals and create meaningful and sustainable change.

In conclusion, the future of social movements under Integral Theory holds great promise for addressing the complex challenges and opportunities facing societies worldwide. By integrating Integral perspectives into their strategies and practices, activists, organizers, and practitioners can gain deeper insights into the dynamics of social change and develop more holistic and effective approaches to promoting justice, equality, sustainability, and well-being for all. As social movements continue to evolve and adapt to changing circumstances, Integral Theory offers a powerful framework for navigating the complexities of collective action and shaping a more just, inclusive, and flourishing future for humanity.

Criticism of Integral Theory

Criticism of Integral Theory arises from various perspectives, highlighting both its strengths and limitations in understanding and addressing complex phenomena. While Integral Theory, developed by philosopher Ken Wilber, offers a comprehensive framework that integrates insights from multiple disciplines, it has faced scrutiny and critique from scholars, practitioners, and critics alike.

One of the primary criticisms of Integral Theory is its perceived complexity and abstract nature. Critics argue that the framework's incorporation of multiple dimensions and perspectives can make it challenging to apply in practical contexts. The extensive terminology and conceptual framework of Integral Theory may also be off-putting to those unfamiliar with its principles, potentially limiting its accessibility and applicability outside of academic circles.

Moreover, some critics question the universality and applicability of Integral Theory across diverse cultural, social, and historical contexts. They argue that Integral Theory, with its emphasis on developmental stages and hierarchical structures, may not adequately account for the diversity of human experiences and perspectives. Critics caution against imposing a singular framework onto complex and multifaceted phenomena, advocating instead for approaches that are more contextually sensitive and culturally inclusive.

Another criticism of Integral Theory pertains to its treatment of spirituality and mysticism. While Integral Theory acknowledges the importance of spiritual dimensions in human experience, some critics argue that it may oversimplify or essentialize complex spiritual traditions. They caution against reducing spirituality to a mere developmental stage or incorporating it into a broader framework without fully appreciating its cultural, historical, and philosophical nuances.

Furthermore, Integral Theory has been criticized for its perceived lack of empirical evidence and scientific rigor. Critics argue that while the framework offers conceptual insights and theoretical models, it may lack empirical support or validation through empirical research. Some scholars contend that Integral Theory's reliance on subjective experiences and introspection may limit its credibility within mainstream academic disciplines.

Additionally, Integral Theory has faced criticism for its perceived hierarchical and elitist tendencies. Critics argue that the framework's emphasis on developmental stages and evolutionary progression may reinforce existing power structures and marginalize alternative perspectives. They caution against adopting a one-size-fits-all approach that privileges certain worldviews or value systems over others, advocating instead for approaches that are more inclusive and egalitarian.

Despite these criticisms, Integral Theory continues to evolve and adapt in response to feedback and debate. Scholars and practitioners within the Integral community actively engage with critiques, refining and expanding the framework to address its limitations and incorporate diverse perspectives. By fostering dialogue and collaboration, Integral Theory seeks to remain relevant and responsive to the complex challenges of the modern world.

In conclusion, while Integral Theory offers valuable insights into the complexities of human experience and social phenomena, it is not without its criticisms. Critics raise valid concerns regarding its complexity, universality, empirical basis, treatment of spirituality, and potential for reinforcing hierarchies. However, Integral Theory's ongoing evolution and engagement with critique demonstrate its commitment to remaining responsive and relevant in addressing the multifaceted challenges of the contemporary world.

Examining Common Criticisms

Integral Theory, developed by philosopher Ken Wilber, has garnered both praise and criticism since its inception. While it offers a comprehensive framework for understanding complex phenomena, it is not immune to scrutiny. Let's delve into some common criticisms leveled against Integral Theory, shedding light on its strengths and limitations.

One frequent criticism of Integral Theory is its perceived complexity and abstraction. Critics argue that its incorporation of multiple dimensions and perspectives can make it challenging to apply in practical contexts. The extensive terminology and conceptual framework may also deter individuals unfamiliar with its principles, limiting its accessibility outside academic circles.

Moreover, some critics question the universality and applicability of Integral Theory across diverse cultural, social, and historical contexts. They argue that its emphasis on developmental stages and hierarchical structures may not fully account for the diversity of human experiences and perspectives. Critics advocate for approaches that are more contextually sensitive and culturally inclusive, cautioning against imposing a singular framework onto complex phenomena.

Integral Theory has also faced criticism regarding its treatment of spirituality and mysticism. While it acknowledges the importance of spiritual dimensions in human experience, critics argue that it may oversimplify or essentialize complex spiritual traditions. Some caution against reducing spirituality to a mere developmental stage or incorporating it into a broader framework without fully appreciating its cultural, historical, and philosophical nuances.

Furthermore, Integral Theory has been criticized for its perceived lack of empirical evidence and scientific rigor. While it offers conceptual insights and theoretical models, some argue that it may lack empirical support or validation through rigorous research. Critics contend that its reliance on subjective experiences and introspection may limit its credibility within mainstream academic disciplines.

Additionally, Integral Theory has been accused of promoting a hierarchical and elitist worldview. Critics argue that its emphasis on developmental stages and evolutionary progression may reinforce existing power structures and marginalize alternative perspectives. They advocate for approaches that are more inclusive and egalitarian, challenging the privileging of certain worldviews or value systems over others.

Despite these criticisms, Integral Theory continues to evolve and adapt in response to feedback and debate. Scholars and practitioners within the Integral community actively engage with critiques, refining and expanding the framework to address its limitations and incorporate diverse perspectives. By fostering dialogue and collaboration, Integral Theory seeks to remain relevant and responsive to the complex challenges of the modern world.

In conclusion, while Integral Theory offers valuable insights into complex phenomena, it is not without its criticisms. Its perceived complexity, universality, treatment of spirituality, empirical basis, and potential for reinforcing hierarchies have all been subjects of critique. However, Integral Theory's ongoing evolution and engagement with critique demonstrate its commitment to remaining responsive and relevant in addressing the multifaceted challenges of the contemporary world.

Response to the Criticism

In response to the criticisms leveled against Integral Theory, proponents of the framework have engaged in ongoing dialogue and reflection to address concerns and refine the approach. While acknowledging the validity of some critiques, advocates of Integral Theory assert its continued relevance and potential for contributing to a deeper understanding of complex phenomena.

One key response to criticism is the acknowledgment of Integral Theory's evolving nature. Proponents emphasize that Integral Theory is not a static framework but a dynamic and open-ended approach that encourages exploration and refinement. They argue that ongoing dialogue and engagement with critique are essential for the continued development and evolution of Integral Theory, allowing it to adapt to changing contexts and incorporate new insights.

Moreover, advocates of Integral Theory emphasize its integrative nature as a strength rather than a weakness. They argue that the framework's incorporation of multiple perspectives and dimensions provides a more comprehensive understanding of complex phenomena. Rather than seeking to reduce complexity, Integral Theory embraces it, recognizing the interconnectedness of various factors and the need for holistic approaches to address them.

In response to concerns about the universality of Integral Theory, proponents highlight its capacity for adaptation and contextualization. They argue that while Integral Theory offers broad principles and frameworks, it can be applied in diverse cultural, social, and historical contexts with appropriate modifications. By engaging with local knowledge systems and incorporating diverse perspectives, Integral Theory can be made more inclusive and relevant to different communities and societies.

Regarding criticisms related to spirituality, proponents of Integral Theory emphasize the importance of nuanced and respectful engagement with spiritual traditions. They acknowledge that spirituality is a complex and multifaceted aspect of human experience that cannot be fully captured by any single framework. However, they argue that Integral Theory provides a useful lens for understanding the role of spirituality in individual and collective development, encouraging dialogue and collaboration between spiritual traditions and other disciplines.

In response to concerns about empirical evidence and scientific rigor, advocates of Integral Theory emphasize the need for a balanced approach that integrates both empirical research and theoretical insight. They acknowledge that while Integral Theory may not always meet the standards of mainstream empirical research, it offers valuable conceptual frameworks and models that can inspire and guide empirical inquiry. By combining theoretical rigor with empirical investigation, Integral Theory can contribute to a more comprehensive understanding of complex phenomena.

Finally, proponents of Integral Theory address criticisms related to hierarchy and elitism by emphasizing the importance of inclusivity and diversity. They argue that Integral Theory is not inherently hierarchical or elitist but can be used in ways that promote equality and justice. By fostering dialogue and collaboration among diverse stakeholders, Integral Theory can help build more inclusive and equitable societies.

In conclusion, while Integral Theory is not immune to criticism, proponents of the framework respond by engaging in ongoing dialogue, reflection, and refinement. By acknowledging the validity of critiques and embracing the dynamic nature of the approach, advocates of Integral Theory seek to address concerns and contribute to its continued development and relevance in addressing the complex challenges of the contemporary world.

Have Questions / Comments?

This book was designed to cover as much as possible but I know I have probably missed something, or some new amazing discovery that has just come out.

If you notice something missing or have a question that I failed to answer, please get in touch and let me know. If I can, I will email you an answer and also update the book so others can also benefit from it.

Thanks For Being Awesome :)

Submit Your Questions / Comments At:

https://xspurts.com/posts/questions

Get Another Book Free

We love writing and have produced a huge number of books.

For being one of our amazing readers, we would love to offer you another book we have created, 100% free.

To claim this limited time special offer, simply go to the site below and enter your name and email address.

You will then receive one of my great books, direct to your email account, 100% free!

https://xspurts.com/posts/free-book-offer